# CHILDREN'S USE OF BOARD GAMES IN PSYCHOTHERAPY

# CHILDREN'S USE OF BOARD GAMES IN PSYCHOTHERAPY

PROPERTY OF
E. JOY MULLER

## JILL BELLINSON

JASON ARONSON INC.
*Northvale, New Jersey*
*London*

This book was set in 13 pt. Centaur by Alabama Book Composition of Deatsville, AL, and printed and bound by Book-Mart Press of North Bergen, NJ.

### Library of Congress Cataloging-in-Publication Data

Bellinson, Jill.
    Taking turns : using board games in child psychotherapy / Jill Bellinson.
       p. ; cm.
    Includes bibliographical references and index.
    ISBN 0–7657–0356–4
       1. Child psychotherapy. 2. Play therapy. 3. Fantasy—Therapeutic use. I. Title.
    [DNLM: 1. Play Therapy—methods—Child. 2. Psychotherapy—methods.
WS 350.2 B444t 2001]
RJ505.P6 .B45 2001
618.92'891653—dc21

                                       2001045976

Printed in the United States of America on acid-free paper. For information and catalog, write to Jason Aronson Inc., 230 Livingston Street, Northvale, NJ 07647-1726, or visit our website: www.aronson.com.

*This book is dedicated to the children who play games:*

*Abigail, Adam, Adena, Alex, Arty, Belinda, Benji, Billy, Carl, Claire, Davida, Debbie, Ellen, Ethan, Francine, Freddie, Gertie, Gregory, Harvey, Ian, Jasmine, Julie, Kal, Kenneth, Kevin, Len, Leroy, Mary, Melissa, Michael, Nadine, Natalie, Patrick, Peter, Richard, Scott, Sonya, Stephanie, Steve, Ted, Tessa, Vinny, Zach, and all those still to come.*

# CONTENTS

This book was over 20 years in the making, beginning in my early training in graduate school. Like so many child therapists, I was taught that board games were best kept out of the playroom, because they led to a shut down of communications rather than an opening to therapeutic interventions. If absolutely necessary, I was told, board games could be introduced with highly resistant children, but only briefly, just long enough to engage the children in treatment— then the games should be hidden away, once the "real" therapy began.

But like so many child therapists, I was repeatedly faced with children who begged for board games, who played them in school and at home, who were not interested in the dramatic play of childhood and who could not yet talk out their difficulties. If not for board games, they would sit fidgeting uncomfortably while I tried unsuccessfully to involve them in fantasy play or—even worse—tortured them with verbal questions. They could not answer my questions, since they were not yet verbal enough to express themselves in those terms, and they experienced themselves as too mature to become absorbed in the dollhouse or action figures most of the time. Their interests—in therapy and outside—were in playing structured games with rules, requirements, and winners.

These children taught me that I had to learn to use board games in their therapy. Structured games, not words and not dramatic play, were their expressive modality. The children I worked with helped me develop ways to use board games in their treatment, and they showed me that this book was necessary, to share my work with other child therapists. I hope the book will prove useful to future therapists, that they might learn more quickly than I did how to speak the board-game language of latency age children.

I am grateful to the children described in the book and the many others I have had the privilege of playing with, for their patience with me as I learned about their world in order to try to help them.

I would also like to thank my teachers and supervisors who allowed me the freedom to explore ideas about board games in therapy, and my supervisees who allowed me to try out my ideas on their captive attention. I am especially grateful to James Gorney, who knew I could write this book before I did; to Joyce Lerner for fostering the early process; and to Ilo Milton, Alison Rosen, and Alan Frosch for their comments during the formative stages. All the staff at Jason Aronson have been unbendingly patient and supportive. I also would like to thank my family for putting up with my absences and my preoccupations while my attention was turned toward the book and away from them.

# CHAPTER ONE

# *Never Use Board Games*

Nine-and-a-half-year-old Richard and I are in the playroom for one of our first few sessions together. He rapidly and almost haphazardly touches several different toys as he moves around the room. He finally settles on the sand table. He hands us dinosaurs, taking the biggest ones for himself, and buries them all the way to their heads in the sand outside the fort he has built. They are pet dinosaurs, he says, but if they get hungry they will bite even us. We will attack them at dawn, while they sleep.

Next there are spacemen in the sand, and monsters. His characters are the toughest and strongest; mine need advice on fort building. Our men fight, die, and come back to life as it quickly becomes "the next century." At the end of the session, after begging for "just a little longer" to play, Richard pockets a tiny monster and leaves the room.

Wait! This book is supposed to be about *board* games! That was a story of dramatic play, not a board game.

It is a scene familiar to most child therapists. Young children play out their fantasies and conflicts in symbolic play like this every day. Most therapists are comfortable attempting interpretations about this kind of play. They see the difficulty Richard has in structuring his play as he moves rapidly from one toy to the next, changing the characters of his stories in the middle. They see the scary monsters he identifies everywhere: in the house, under the sand, from outer space. They see the family pet that turns dangerous even toward loved ones if it becomes too needy, and the aggressive orality of that neediness. They see the phallic competition for the biggest and best, which he wins for himself, needing to see himself as bigger and stronger and more knowledgeable about fort building than his therapist. They see the unpredictability of his world in the beloved pet that can turn on him, the attack during a trusting sleep, the impermanence of even death. They see his neediness and his need to hide it in the way he surreptitiously steals a toy before he leaves the room. And there are dozens of other thoughts and feelings expressed and interpretations of those dynamics, which could be an entire chapter themselves.

This book is an attempt to demonstrate the way the themes one sees in dramatic play emerge in structured game play as well, because children show themselves in everything they play and do. Structured games allow the same window into unconscious dynamics as dramatic play provides for younger children and dream work provides for adolescents and adults, if one can learn to look at structured games in this way.

The games discussed here are any structured games with specific rules of interaction; they include board games, card games, dominoes, and many sports and even electronic and computer games. When board games are mentioned, it refers to any of these structured games.

## LITERATURE ON PLAY

The literature on child therapy (e.g., Axline, 1969; Bromfield, 1997; Chethik, 1989; A. Freud, 1946; Glenn, 1978; Haworth, 1964; Klein, 1932; Moustakas, 1970; Slade & Wolf, 1994; Spiegel, 1996; Winnicott, 1977) is full of descriptions of working with dramatic play. In the 1987 edition of *The Psychoanalytic Study of the Child*, (Solnit & Neubauer, 1987) 12 articles were devoted to discussion of the meanings of play such as that mentioned above.

These descriptions of interpretation of dramatic play, though, tend to be about fairly young children. The examples in the articles in *Psychoanalytic Study of the Child* are for the most part of children age 2 to 6, with only one clearly regressed child of 8 in more than 200 pages of discussion.

But my practice in child psychotherapy has a lot of 9- and 10-year-olds in it. They tend not to play out so dramatically, and they certainly do not talk, like an adolescent or adult might. They are primarily at the shrugging, silent, "Fine," "Nothing" stage of communication.

They do play board games, though. And we want them to. A 10- or 11-year old who continued to play exclusively in the dollhouse or with action figures would strike us as infantile, regressed. As Oedipal issues fade and children enter the years of latency, it is expected that they will begin to repress active expression of conflicts and acquire sublimation. They have to become able to sit still in school, attend to their lessons, delay their own gratification for that of others, share, refrain from or at least postpone direct expression of their impulses—in short, live in harmony in society (Sarnoff, 1976). It is true that most child patients are referred for treatment precisely because they cannot succeed at some of these tasks. But a latency-age prepubescent child who could perform none of these socially expected behaviors would be cause for concern.

The tasks of latency (Peller, 1954; Sarnoff, 1976) include a lessening need for magical thinking, an increasing capacity to work, and the developing capacity for the internalization of social values. The play of latency (Peller, 1954) includes more socializing, competitiveness, interest in fair play, and ego structure. This means that latency-age children use less symbolic play—direct motoric expression and magical thinking—and more structured, rule-oriented play. As Oedipal children develop into latency, then, there is a decrease in their dramatic play and a concomitant increase in the structure of their games.

I followed this process with Claire, a 10-year-old girl who entered therapy unable to play structured games and absorbed in symbolic play with dollhouse and farm animals. One day she became curious about the Clue game, took out the box, opened the board, and set up the game pieces. She then moved the pieces into various rooms and created play for them— eating in the dining room, dancing in the ballroom, reading in the library, conversing with each other. Gradually, she began to wonder about the box-top rules of the game and started tossing dice to move around the board . . . before moving back to dramatic play when her pieces were in each game room. Over the course of several months she expressed more and more interest in the way her age-mates played the game and gradually developed an ability to play in a structured way rather than a dramatic one.

As her therapist, I found it easier to understand her dynamic issues when her characters fed the animals on the farm, or threatened to move out when the farmer treated them badly, or cut their fingers while cooking for everyone in the Boddy Mansion of the Clue game. However, I also worried that this play was too infantile for a more-than-10-year-old, who ought to be ready to enter a more work-oriented world and begin to prepare emotionally for adolescence. The structured game of Clue was more appropriate for the development of these future stages of life. While I would not have forced her to play a board game as a way to press her into adolescence, I would not want to prevent her maturation by trying to retain her at the stage of dramatic play. She was moving on developmentally—and appropriately—and I needed to move on with her.

So we want our 10-year-olds to play board games, but we need methods of understanding the psychodynamics that may not seem to be as clearly visible in these games.

## LITERATURE ON BOARD GAMES

As flooded as the literature is with articles describing the uses of dramatic play, there is a drought of information about board games; there must be fewer than a dozen articles, most of them derogatory. Earl Loomis (1964) wrote one of the earliest papers about the use of checkers, one of the only papers in praise of board games, in which he suggested games as a way to discover the presence and meanings of resistances and character problems. Other than Loomis' classic paper, most articles that mention structured games at all see them as having very limited value. Richard Gardner (1993) considers checkers "relatively low in therapeutic efficiency" (p. 247), because he sees the game as such a poor expressive medium, and he considers chess "far lower."

Authors who do see any use for structured games use them solely for observation: observation of pathology (R. Gardner, 1993; Johnson, 1993), character style (R. Gardner, 1993; Loomis, 1964), resistances (Loomis, 1964), self-esteem (J. Gardner, 1993; R. Gardner, 1993; Meeks, 1970), expression of aggressiveness (Johnson, 1993; Levinson, 1976; Loomis, 1964), and problem-solving skills (J. Gardner, 1993). They are seen primarily as methods of observing a child's response to competition (R. Gardner, 1993; Loomis, 1964; Smith, 1993) or loss (R. Gardner, 1993; Levinson, 1976; Loomis, 1964; Meeks, 1970), or the child's ability to experience fun (R. Gardner, 1993) or test reality (Levinson, 1976; Meeks, 1970). Games are seen as clearly adjunctive to treatment (R. Gardner, 1993; Levinson, 1976; Loomis, 1964) rather than as constituting the treatment itself. The treatment available in structured games is only in "altering inappropriate attitude[s]" (R. Gardner, 1993, p. 251), managing cheating, developing better coping skills (Johnson, 1993; Meeks, 1970), or as a teaching instrument (J. Gardner, 1993; R. Gardner, 1993; Johnson, 1993).

Some writers have described treatment taking place over the top of a game board. This is similar to what might happen between two adult friends who have an ongoing chess game spanning the course of weeks or months—one moves, they chat a little about life and work and love, the other moves, they talk some more, their time together is over, and they continue again another day. Masud Khan (1983) describes an adult patient he treated this way using a backgammon game; the game served as a conflict-free area in the therapy process, a relief from the talking cure that was going on around it.

Games can be useful this way for noncommunicative adults or especially for adolescents, who often need a retreat from painful talk, but this book is about a different use for games. This is about a treatment in which psychodynamics are seen in the game itself, the way they might in dollhouse play or a scene created with action figures. While there are a few authors (cf., e.g., Coriat, 1941; Fried, 1992; Smith, 1993) who have analyzed the game of chess for the Oedipal meanings inherent in the game itself, there is very little discussion of any other structured games as sources of unconscious dynamics. While this book was in preparation, the newly created Journal of Infant, Child, and Adolescent Psychotherapy published a panel of papers (Bellinson, 2000; Herman, 2000; Krimendahl, 2000; Meeks, 2000) about board games, and particularly cheating at board games. This included Meeks' (2000) commentary discussing his earlier paper (Meeks, 1970) and the critical comments (Beiser, 1970) about that paper, which was not well received in the child therapy community.

One of the reasons so many experts have seen structured games as nonuseful is because of their concentration on the content of the games themselves. If one looks only at the moves prescribed in the games—throw the dice, pick a card, count the spaces, pay the money, go to jail—there do seem to be very few observable dynamics available. This has led therapists to use games created specifically for therapeutic purposes, such as the Talking, Feeling, Doing Game, (Gardner, 1973), the Interactional Analysis Game

(Oden, 1976), the Ungame (Zalick, 1975), and Gardner's various approaches to resistant children (Gardner, 1975). These games structure the play so that it elicits information about the child outside the therapy. As such, they can certainly be very useful. But finding out about the child's life is of only limited use in child treatment, because we still have to find ways to use the information in therapeutic ways for the child.

It might even be argued that one can do treatment without knowing anything about the life events of a patient. A child whose dollhouse father yells and screams and hits everyone in the house, then breaks furniture and storms out while mom hides in the bathroom, is a child who lives with a dominant, angry father figure and a frightened, inadequate mother figure. One does not need to hear life details to understand that clearly from the dramatic play. One does need ways to understand game play as clearly in order to enter into the game play to help the therapeutic process take place. Latency-age children do play board games; their therapists have to learn to make use of this common, expectable mode of interaction.

## EXAMPLES OF GAME PLAY

Let us go back to Richard, the sandbox player described above. In his dramatic play with dinosaurs, he showed his short attention span, his fear that hostile creatures were waiting everywhere to defeat him, his strong dependency needs, his need to have the biggest and the best, as well as his attempt to demonstrate that he had skills that his therapist lacked. Later in his treatment, Richard progressed into latency and structured game play. He showed a particular interest in chess, a game that a teenage uncle had taught him but that he—of course—always lost and always felt inadequate about. Here is a vignette of his chess play after he had introduced the game a week or two earlier:

It is maybe eight moves into the game, just beginning to move toward confrontation. Richard is impatient. "You take too long. . . . if you don't move in ten seconds, I'm gonna move for you. . . . ten. . . . nine. . . . eight, seven, six, five, four, three, two, one, zero, aaanh, you lose," and he moves for me—an inconsequential pawn on the far side of the board. He then makes his own move, closer to the game battle. "See what happens? You have to pay attention or you're gonna lose the game." I remark about how hard it is to keep up with someone as fast as he is, that the move "I" made looked like a really bad one—not as good as his move—and that he was going to be sure to win this game. "Now you're talking so much you're gonna lose your move again," he says. "Come *on*." I think a moment. "I get another move since you're so slow." And he takes my bishop. He then goes on to take four or five moves to every one of mine. "I win. No wonder I win, you don't even know how to play this game. All you do is talk all the time, how do you ever expect to win?"

This vignette shows the same dynamics seen in the sandbox episode, now in board-game play. He has the same short attention span, shown here by his inability to wait for his opponent to move. (Please note that I am no Bobby Fischer. This was not world-class chess we were playing, and I was not waiting my regulation hour between moves. I knew a little more chess than he did at this point in our work, far less than he did when we completed our work a year or so later and he had continued to develop his skills. I needed under a minute to contemplate the board each time, mostly to calculate which spaces my knight could occupy.)

Richard could not sit still long enough to wait. He certainly could not contain his anxiety—perhaps his old fear that hostile creatures were waiting to defeat him, this time in the board game. The hostile creatures on the chessboard were his uncle and his therapist, both trusted and loved until he felt we turned on him like his fantasized pet dinosaurs did. He needed to be the best here as well as in the sandbox. Again he had to teach me the basic information that he had and I lacked—not fort building in this session but chess playing and the proper timing of moves. His impulsiveness can be seen in the way he acted out his anxieties over my move and his inability to gain back his control after his first cheat during the game. He "stole" this game in the same forbidden way he pocketed a creature from the sandbox before leaving the playroom earlier. The same processes can be seen in both the sandbox and the board game.

Richard's need for battle had been clear from early in his treatment. When my sandbox team wanted not to fight but to spend some time in the comfortable house he built for us, his team threatened to blow up all of New York City if we would not fight. When we started play on the same team of good-guys-versus-bad-guys, he arranged for me to betray him so he had to start shooting against me instead of with me. He consistently asked for or attempted to steal privileges I had to say no to: more time in the playroom, toys to take home with him, going home with me, sharing his session with the child after us in the playroom, and so on. His chess playing showed the same dynamics, both in his need to cheat and in the insistent, expressive way in which he did so. Outside sessions, he was almost uncontrollable in the way he demanded special treatment—not wearing his seat belt on the school bus, for example, or not being required to go to reading classes—and there he acted out aggressively when he was refused it. In his therapy sessions he displayed these dynamics symbolically, both in his dramatic play and in his chess games.

## SECOND SET OF EXAMPLES

Here is another pair of examples of Richard's play, dramatic and then on the chessboard, that demonstrates another set of parallel dynamics:

In dramatic play:

We are going to play "Guns." We are police officers. Richard makes me a "lady cop" and puts money and a gun in the purse I am to carry. Then he announces that he is the only cop, that I robbed a bank, the money in my purse proves it, and he will have to arrest me. Then he gives me more money, takes it back, gives it again, and takes it back. We play argue, shoot each other, and come back to life several times. At the end of the session, he throws money all over the room for me to clean up, grabs a small toy, and runs out of the room.

On the chess board:

We are going to properly decide who goes first, Richard says. He puts a pawn in each hand behind his back and asks me to pick. I discover a black pawn (black goes last), and he then shows me that he had black in both hands, so he was guaranteed to go first. He starts moving slowly and fairly, then takes several moves in a row before I get to move at all. He undoes the move I do make and moves a different piece of mine. He moves several times, waits for me to move, and begins the sequence again. He accomplishes checkmate quickly, but clears the board and starts a new game as if he had not won. When we have only 1 minute left in the session, he moves to checkmate and leaves the room.

These are, again, similar dynamics. Richard sets up fair play, with both of us working together, then betrays me by changing the rules behind my back—or *his* back, literally, in the chess game. He reverses his trickery repeatedly during both episodes, not able to fully win, but also not able to allow fair play to take its course. The end of the session brings about enough anger at me, or freedom from repercussions, that he defeats me fully and leaves. In each episode, he has tried out fair play but has been unable to maintain it, defeating himself as well as me.

So it can be seen that the structured games that are developmentally appropriate to latency-age children can reveal a child's unconscious dynamics as well as dramatic play can for younger children or dream work can for adolescents and adults. As therapists, we can search for the same underlying dynamics we would look for in these other symbolic expressions.

Latency-age children generally achieve a stage of development where they replace the dramatic, magical play of childhood with the structured, rule-oriented play of the middle years. In order to be successful therapists for children at this age, we must follow them in this development rather than try to force them to continue with the more regressed play of childhood or to push them prematurely into the verbal world of adolescents and adults. If we watch for them, we can understand unconscious content, defensive needs, and interpersonal and transferential relationships in free play with structured games, just as well as with other symbolic material.

# CHAPTER TWO

# *Always Use Board Games*

Kenneth, a small 4½-year-old, pulls his chair over to the toy cabinet, climbs on it, and stands on tiptoe in order to reach the top of the top shelf, where the boxes of board games are kept. Although he cannot yet read and he plays at home with action figures and construction toys, in the office he is interested only in the structured games on the top shelf. He takes down Say It With Clay—a kind of Pictionary charades game played with Play-Doh. He sets up the board, spins the spinner, deals out cards, and then suggests that we make towers of the three colors of chips to see if we can make them high, compare their sizes, and knock them over.

Kenneth's interest in board games is slightly premature. It is an interest that is more likely to develop in an older child, reading or ready to start reading. Most 4½-year-olds have more need for a physical outlet and more interest in dramatic play. In his outside life,

Kenneth was generally no exception. In the office, however, he showed an unusually precocious interest in the structure of games.

In the previous chapter, I discussed the absence of detailed discussion of board games in the psychotherapy literature. Nevertheless, the ability to use board games is an important developmental step for children, one that is often acquired during the years a child is in treatment. Therapists can often follow children's progress in accepting the structure, rules, and restrictions that board games provide as the children acquire the capacity for fair play. Claire, described in Chapter 1, is an example of this, as is Kenneth.

In his board games, Kenneth showed a pattern parallel to that shown during the rest of his time in my office. He seemed to vacillate between an attempt to be strong, calm, focused, and mature, and giving way to a wild, regressed excitement. He would sit at the table, describing his experiences during the week, and by the end of the story he would be standing and running and jumping around the room, unable to contain his excitement over the tale of his adventures. In dollhouse play, characters would start by sitting down to dinner or television watching and end by climbing to the roof to scream while jumping or throwing people off.

Kenneth's use of structured games was similar: His interests in them at all was an advanced statement, an attempt to be calm, focused, and mature, choosing materials that were obviously meant for taller children who could reach the top shelf and who could read and follow directions. He wanted to reach them himself, even if it meant standing on tiptoe, reaching above his head, and dropping materials when he couldn't fully hold on. He set up the board, using visual cues and answers from me to his questions about customary play. He asked for help reading words printed on the board or cards or equipment. As in his other play, the extended effort would be too difficult, however, and he would eventually become wilder and more regressed. He would abandon the structure of the game, replacing it with tower building or card matching, and eventually becoming overcome with excitement and the need for physical outlet.

Kenneth pulls Clue down from the top shelf, spilling the contents and nearly dropping the box as he tries to drag it down from where he can barely reach it. He sets up the board, asking which color piece starts at which assigned square around the outside edges. He takes out and labels each weapon, deciding carefully where to place each of them at the outset. He looks at each card, matches it to its equivalent on the board, and slips it into the Solution envelope, which he places with great ceremony in the center of the board—an unsatisfactory placement, since it covers the staircase that Kenneth feels is necessary to get upstairs to bedrooms or down to secret passageways. Then he picks up the Revolver and pretends to shoot it—at the walls, ceiling, toy closet. He takes the Lead Pipe and balances it carefully on the Candlestick, then throws it at the Candlestick when it falls over. He then throws the other weapons at and across the board, then across the room, shouting and jumping as he does so.

Kenneth's behavior as he tells a story, his dollhouse play, and his structured game play all reveal the same struggle between his wish for maturity and control, and his uncontainable excitement and need for physical expression. These were also his presenting problems: while he was clearly extremely bright and functioning well in the academic aspects of school, he was often out of control and overly physical both at school and at home.

Kenneth's use of board games demonstrated his psychological functioning, as game play usually does, but it also demonstrated a typical stage in the evolution of structured game play for most children. Young children play dramatically with dolls and trucks and dress-up toys, action figures and tea sets and construction materials; adolescents play fully structured, rule-determined games of chess and cards and backgammon, Scrabble and Boggle and Go. In between lies the development of the interest in and the ability to follow rules of play.

Kenneth showed a somewhat early interest in structured games, needing to seem mature for his age. He then used them age appropriately for a 4-year-old. His mature intellectual skills led him to develop strong one-to-one correspondence abilities at an early age. He could count accurately very well for his age. However, he was still not able to sustain the structure of the game for long, and he was not at all ready to sublimate. He—like Claire—could not use the metaphor of the game expressively. The Revolver could not be a symbol of a revolver, the Dining Room could not be a picture of a room to count in and out of. Both Kenneth and Claire had to use the gun to shoot and the dining room to feed and be fed. For Kenneth, the tension between his need for a high level of maturity and his inability to sustain that level overwhelmed him each session, leading him to lose track of the game structure altogether.

Kenneth takes one card at a time out of the Solution envelope in which he has placed them all. He draws Colonel Mustard. He looks for him, first on the boxtop picture, then in the set of colored playing pieces. He is upset that the colors don't match—the yellow pawn is unlike the gold of the card or the brown on the box top. He then draws the Conservatory card,

18

finds the room on the board, and places Colonel Mustard there. Mrs. White—in the Lounge—calls to Colonel Mustard to join her, through the secret passage. Kenneth sends characters through the board's secret passages, then creates his own to the other rooms in the mansion. Then he makes a secret passage across the office—the actual room we are sitting in—and sends characters to the bookcase, the desk, and the telephone table. He gets wilder and wilder, until all the characters and all the equipment are strewn around the corners of the office, and Kenneth is jumping and shouting with excitement.

As he matures, we expect that Kenneth will acquire the ability to maintain the structure of the game longer, to use the squares of the board rather than the corners of the office for movement, to "kill" Mr. Boddy in fantasy rather than the action figures on the roof or the real people he gets angry at. We, as therapists, will have to acquire the ability to understand him in his structured game play as well as his more directly expressed fantasies.

From all that has been said so far, it can be seen that the structured games that are developmentally appropriate to latency-age children can reveal a child's unconscious dynamics as well as dramatic play can for younger children or dream work can for adolescents and adults. It must be allowed to unfold in the same free-floating way that dramatic play or dream reports would flow, and we should search for the same underlying dynamics we would look for in these other symbolic expressions. Any method of game play can be seen and interpreted in this light.

So what should be done with the material uncovered in game play? Just what would be done with symbolic material uncovered through any method of discovery. Understanding this kind of work transcends any particular school of thought. One can work with drive derivatives, self-psychology, or interpersonal or relational theory as expressed in structured games. Interpretations can be metaphoric or direct, in children's play as well as in children's game play.

Here are some examples of the way I work with these games, starting with ways I do not work with them.

## USE OF GAMES: DON'TS

First, I do not introduce board games because I do not introduce any materials into the play. I have available a variety of play and art materials, including dolls, action figures, puppets, cars, blocks, Play-Doh, crayons, and a variety of structured board games. While I see structured game play as a necessary developmental step for latency-age children to make and dramatic play as regressive for them, I do not introduce board games in order to stem that regression. Children in treatment with me choose their materials as they wish. I see my job as observing what is revealed in their choices, and interpreting.

The choice of games itself is interesting to note:

> Kenneth begins every session with a climb to the games at the top of the top shelf, far beyond his young reach. Mary, a childish girl of about the same age, begins her sessions with a game of hide-and-seek—a barely disguised version of peek-a-boo.

Harvey plays every game in the cabinet, but only once. Melissa plays Uno, over and over again, every session all session. Richard explores all the games until he discovers chess, which he then plays exclusively.

Billy, like many children with aggression difficulties, likes Sorry—especially when we rename it Not-Sorry!

Patrick creates his own game—something like Monopoly, using buildings and stores in his therapist's neighborhood.

In the simple act of choosing a game, these children show some aspect of their personality. Kenneth demonstrates his attempts at hypermaturity, while Mary shows regressive tendencies. Harvey cannot stick to a game while Melissa cannot change her game, and Richard explores until he finds his niche. Billy chooses a game that expresses his real-life conflict over behaving badly and the apology that so many adults seem to require of him. Patrick hates external structure, so refuses to use any game that imposes this on him—but uses his strong creativity to develop an alternative method of working out his conflicts about rules. Permitting these children to make their choice of game—or activity other than games—allows me to understand and interpret this aspect of their characters.

There is one exception to this general rule of child choice. I do edit the materials I make available slightly, based on my own needs. I do not keep finger paints, for example. There are those who feel they represent an important opportunity for expression of regressive, anal play for those children who need it. I have discovered that for me this rarely works. The children who seem to "need" to get their hands dirty are those who most avoid the Play-Doh that is in my office. The children who smash other children's toys and block towers in their schools rarely choose the building blocks in my office; I have Blockhead available—a game of piling up odd-shaped wooden pieces until they fall over—but the very children I expect to like to play the game are the least likely to choose it. In any event, I do not keep finger paints in my office because I do not want to clean up the mess; other media are available to express similar dynamics of regression and messiness. There are a few structured games, too, which I find I myself prefer not to play. These, too, are not on my shelves; this will be discussed further in Chapter 8.

The only materials that I find really cannot be used as part of treatment are electronic games. While they can be used as icebreakers or can be informative about a child's character style (Zelnick, 1999), they do not lend themselves to ongoing therapeutic work as other structured games do. This is because it is difficult, if not impossible, to play against the rules. Some of these games have hints or shortcuts one can use, or ways to replay the game from some previous point, or unlimited "lives" to allow a player to go on at great length, but they generally cannot be manipulated in the ways that nonautomated games can. I leave it to future writers to describe ways to play creatively with these games, or to discover ways to use these games as adequate projective material in other ways; I have not found ways for them to be therapeutically useful as expressive media.

I cannot always control the games we play, because children sometimes bring in their own games to play. This is especially true for electronic games. If a child does bring in an electronic game, I try to make whatever use of it as I can. Since I do not direct what my child patients play with or how they play with the materials I provide, I also do not direct their play with their own materials.

Child-provided material is sometimes an expression of their disappointment with the materials in my playroom—in which case I try to oblige by adding to my supply. This is the reason Barbie dolls made their way into my toy closet! Sometimes children who bring their own toys are showing me that they are never satisfied with anything they encounter in life—in which case I try to interpret that experience. And sometimes, particularly with electronic games, children are demonstrating their conflict over being with me at all, because their absorption in the game often excludes me. In this case, I try to understand the meaning of excluding me:

> Ethan brings his own Gameboy. He parks himself on the floor with his back to his therapist and plays his game in silence.

> Ted brings in his electronic Pokemon Game and the book of documentation to accompany it. He sits in a chair—the chair I sit in when I work with adults—and reads the book, then plays the game. He does not acknowledge my presence.

While the apparent play of these two children was similar, they were in fact communicating very different psychological experiences. In Ethan's case, there had been a meeting during the previous week between his therapist and his father—an angry, punitive, critical parent—in which Ethan imagined his therapist had sided with his father. He was expressing his anger at his therapist's recent behavior, which he interpreted as a betrayal. An examination of the events that had transpired between the two during and since the last session—first silently on the part of Ethan's therapist, then aloud for Ethan's benefit—allowed discovery of the meaning of Ethan's use of this solitary game brought from home. He then put the game away and joined his therapist in his usual, more connected, modes of relating.

A similar examination in Ted's case could not uncover any specific instances of potential anger at the therapist. Ted, however, is a child whose presenting problem was a difficulty in social relations and a tendency to withdraw. So while the reason for this specific withdrawal was not clear, I approached the situation as an opportunity to understand Ted's ongoing difficulties. I asked if I could sit where I could watch him play; this question was designed for me to explore whether he meant to actively exclude me from his world or was simply relating in his usual solitary way. While Ted often answers my queries with angry exhortations—indicating an active and angry exclusion—this time he agreed that I could place a chair behind him so I could see his game. (I have to admit that I was also curious about the game itself; this was in the early days of the fleeting popularity of this electronic game, and I had not seen what it looked like. So I was doubly pleased when he allowed me to watch him.) I watched him in silence briefly, impressed by his agility and knowledge of the game, commenting on this and my genuine inability to even see the game well, let alone play it. Some children offer to let me try their game at this point; Ted only grunted his contempt for my incompetence. Soon, however, he began to comment under his breath about how well he was doing or where he was going next. I asked him further questions about his performance and his decisions, and he explained further nuances of the game until falling back to his silent pursuit of his lonely activity.

In both of these cases, the solitary, enforced-rule electronic games these children brought into their therapy from their homes did allow exploration of the issues on their minds, albeit limited. Ethan's behavior with his game could be understood as expression of his anger at his therapist, and therefore his exclusion of this therapist and even his therapy hour from his play. The solitary play with his electronic game represented a metaphor for Ethan's angry wish to exclude his therapist from his life. After this meaning was interpreted to him, Ethan went on to play more inclusive games, as had been his custom.

Ted's behavior with his game was understood as communicating something different. After anger at recent behavior of the therapist was considered, to no avail, his game playing was understood as an expression of longer-term, more deeply seated character issues of social isolation. The game could then be understood as a metaphor for all Ted's relations: He created a world of his own, invited me in to be a part of it briefly, then retreated to solitary play when the connection became too intense for him. After alone time to recuperate his psychic strength, he invited my participation again, and again retreated when he needed to. The structure of this game, rather than the content, served as the vehicle for the connect—disconnect therapeutic work that Ted needed to do with me.

So while I think that electronic games have limited usefulness in psychotherapy, they are not entirely without meaning, and when they are unavoidable, such as when children bring in games from home or when they discover the computer games available on the desktop computers in our offices (Zelnick, 1999), we should attempt to make what use of them we can. As with other board games, children of a certain age and developmental stage begin to play with these games; we expect them to, so we have to be able to work therapeutically with them when they do.

Lastly, although I expect that children will use games creatively rather than according to box-top rules—that is, I expect they will cheat (see Chapter 4)—I do not manipulate my own play so as to allow a child to win or lose—that is, do not cheat. If a child sets up a structured game, I read it as a sign that he or she is ready to begin the tasks of latency. I will play dramatically, as Kenneth and Claire did, until the child introduces rule play. At that point I play fairly, according to rules, no matter how the child asks me to cheat. Children often give me permission to move backward, or roll a second time, or use a secret passageway that does not exist, or start on the wrong square like they do, but I do not accept the offer or alter my play. I attend to psychodynamics rather than paying attention to the game strategy itself, so I am usually not playing my very best, but I do not intentionally play in order to cheat or to let the child win.

## USE OF GAMES: DO'S

How do I use games? As I watch for revelation of projective material in the way a child relates to the game and the way "cheating" unfolds, I attempt to bring this information to the attention of the playing child. In the War game described above or in Richard's chess game in Chapter 1, I discussed the cheating as it began but did not attempt to control it. This is in contrast to authors (Agre, 1997b; J. Gardner, 1993; R. Gardner, 1975, 1993) who stop cheating immediately or those (Meeks, 1970) who believe cheating should be watched and allowed to unfold first and then be questioned. I do not ever confront it or try to prevent it; I just discuss it.

In the first chess example in this book, for example, I talked to Richard about how hard it was for him to wait for me to move, not knowing whether I was going to put him in a losing position or not. I talked about how stupid "I" was to move the inconsequential pawn when there were pieces of mine much more important to pay attention to. I discussed his ability to win—and his need to

26

win—no matter what it took. I said I thought it must feel good for him to win and be awfully important to him if he needed to take so many extra moves to do so. I continued to talk about how hard it was for him to sit still and wait to see what might happen, how afraid he was of the worst, how he could at least control the outcome of the game by playing the way he did. I could also have mentioned the parallel with experiences he had with his mother and teachers and bus drivers in his outside life, or how painful it was for him to feel he was losing any battle he fought—with learning to read, for example.

I did not make any attempt to stop his extra moves, or move faster next time so he would not have time for cheating, or block him from moving my pieces. Nor did I discuss the proper way to play the game. I knew his uncle did enough of this at home, and his classmates refused to play with him when he cheated; he did not need me for that. I thought that the way I could help him was by trying to tolerate his need to impulsively win and to help him understand where that need came from and what it led to. If I had tried to stop his behavior, it would have led only to a power struggle over his moves, not a better understanding of them. Rather, I watched him and commented on the way he played:

R: HURRY UP!!!!

JB: It's really hard for you to wait for me to make my move.

R: Yeah, Now COME ON!!!

JB: You're not sure what I might do if I take a long time to think. I might find a way to get you to lose, and then you'd feel bad.

R: You're still talking. You're not moving. I'm gonna move your piece.

27

(He moves my pawn on the outer edge of the board, then takes my bishop.)

*JB:* Boy, I sure did a dumb thing there. If I didn't protect my bishop, you were going to take it, and I made a stupid move to not protect it. I must be a really bad chess player if I thought that was the right move. I guess I'm really stupid about this. No wonder I always lose and you always win.

*R:* You're talking again. MOVE!

*JB:* And now it's hard to wait again, in case I think up a better move this time. You're really worried you might not win this game. You hate it when you don't win.

(I move, placing his knight—a cherished piece—in jeopardy.)

*R:* You're so slow, I'm just gonna take all the moves. (He proceeds to move his own pieces, one after another, taking all mine off the board without allowing me to make any moves of my own. He leaves only my king, which he tips over in defeat.)

*JB:* Wow! Here I thought I was going to take your knight, but you couldn't let that happen. You took *all* the moves after that. Not only didn't I get your knight, I didn't get anything after that. That'll serve me right for trying to take something you wanted. You really got me back—you killed me.

*R:* Nobody threatens me and gets away with it! I win! I win! I always win!

*JB:* You do always win. That's the most important thing for you; you have to win or you feel awful.

In this example, I described Richard's play as he demonstrated it: his inability to wait, his fear of losing self-esteem, his decimating my team when I appeared to threaten his most important game piece. I also commented on reasons I understood for his playing in this way:

his worry that I might be too successful, his need to win every time, his feeling inadequate when he loses, his needing to strike back with enormous force when someone threatens his cherished objects. In describing "my" stupidity for making bad moves, I was attempting to describe how I thought he feels when he makes poor decisions about his own play, when he loses to his uncle, when he is unable to succeed at any of the tasks he attempts. Through the play and my describing it metaphorically, I hoped to show Richard that I understood some of what went on inside him and wanted to understand even more. I wanted him to feel that I was most interested in his emotional experiences—not in which of us won or lost—and that whatever he felt was acceptable.

In time, I also remarked about his bringing himself to the brink of winning and then failing to checkmate me. By the time I did this, Richard was able to talk to me about his play, not tell me to shut up and move already, but describe some of his experiences. He said that checkmating was not interesting to him; he did not feel he had won the game unless he had removed all the opponent's pieces—the same decimation he showed in sandbox and cops-and-robbers play.

I could talk with him then about his feeling so inadequate that he needed to massacre the opponent to feel even a little bit success-ful himself. I could suggest that he might enjoy playing so much that he wanted to stretch the game out as long as possible, or that his fear of losing might be a bit exciting for him.

I worked with Richard's psychodynamics through the meta-phor of his chess playing. He is worried about his own inadequacies everywhere, not just on the chessboard: He feels inadequate when he loses at real chess to his uncle, when he cannot read no matter how hard he tries, when he has a hard time getting himself ready for school in the morning. Each setback devastates him, so he devastates his opponent in a creative chess game. The worry about a setback makes him so anxious that he cannot bear to wait for what might happen next, in life and in the game. My pointing this out to Richard helps him become aware of what worries him and how he responds to anxiety, and thus helps him gain more control of his actions. It offers me as an understanding helper, a confidante for his anxieties and a calm discussant who knows what he feels but is not devastated by it.

My doing all this within the metaphor of the game allows him to play out his difficulties and the potential solutions in a nonthreatening, age-appropriate environment. Richard did not directly tell me that his reading failures frighten him, so I did not directly talk with him about his reading failures; he did not say he loses his self-esteem when he feels his mother does not care for him, so I did not say this loss increased his fidgetiness. He played his anxiety on the game board; I described his anxiety on the game board. He eventually became less anxious on the game board, and then in his life.

There are other possible interpretations as well, and other ways to work with this material. For instance, there was no father or consistent male rival in Richard's life, so killing off the king may not have been important to him. I did not feel the need to interpret to Richard outside the metaphor of the game; he expressed himself on the chessboard, and I worked with his dynamics on the chessboard, seeing it as transferential. There is no reason it should not be interpreted to him this way, it is just not my preferred way to work.

As we played together, Richard began to talk more and more about his game play. He described his feelings as he won, lost, or decimated the field, and he began to talk about the cheating itself. He clearly enjoyed the play with me, reveling in his blatantly illegal moves and making them with great drama, criticizing me relentlessly for my "incompetence." Meanwhile, his play outside the therapy became much more controlled; he stopped cheating with his outside partners, and stopped his angry tantrums when he lost to them. This seems to be the equivalent of a transference neurosis: his game-playing symptoms flourished in the therapy room and diminished in his outside life.

This newfound ability to play fairly outside the therapy was important to him, and productive. He had more friends and play-mates because he was more fun to be with, and he was able to acquire many more skills on the chessboard, since he had to find ways to defeat his outside opponents using real chess strategies. He also developed some insight into the importance of our work. He told me that he was able to play "the right way" with his uncle and friends and "our way" with me. Before our summer break, he expressed his concern that he would lose this ability. In our last session before the break, as he wished "ten o'clock would never come, because then we could stay in the playroom forever," he worried to me that he would have no one to play with over the summer, because he would not be able to play "our way" with anybody until I came back, and so he would not have the strength to play correctly, and all his friends would desert him.

Not only had Richard developed the ego strength to control his own play, he also came to understand the connection between his unruly behavior and the way his peers treated him. This was an impressive insight for a disturbed, previously highly disruptive 10-year-old, and he developed it in play therapy that evolved, with his own development, through dramatic play into structured game play. My play with him paralleled his development, and I watched and interpreted the dynamics revealed in the ways he played in either modality.

Richard's treatment is an example of the ways in which we can understand psychodynamics through structured games as well as dramatic play, and the way in which a child can change through treatment on a chessboard.

# CHAPTER THREE

# Not Ordinary Games: The Use of Specially Designed Therapeutic Games

Steve picks a new game off the toy shelf. We set up the board, choose colors, and throw the dice to see who goes first. Steve wins. He rolls, counts his squares, and lands on "Go back 2." He counts back two spaces and lands on a white square. He picks a white card, reads it silently, looks up at me and says, "Hey, this is no ordinary board game!"

Steve was playing the Talking, Feeling, and Doing Game (Gardner, 1973). The white card had asked him to tell what he thought of a boy who curses at his father. While we had played many games with instruction cards before, he was quick to realize that these cards and this game were different. This game was created specifically for therapeutic purposes, probably due to the frustrations experienced by so many child therapists when they find that latency-age children respond well to the structure of board games but poorly to attempts to get them to talk directly.

This chapter will describe the use of these specially designed games, such as the Talking, Feeling, Doing Game (Gardner, 1973), the Interactional Analysis Game (Oden, 1976), the Ungame (Zalick, 1975), and Gardner's various approaches to resistant children (Gardner, 1975).

Therapeutic games structure the play so that it elicits information about the child outside the therapy. They all include some elements of typical structured play: Players take turns, roll dice, pick cards or pieces of paper or toy objects, and usually win or lose rounds. In the meantime, the games require children to describe or play out some aspect of their lives or fantasies, and allow the therapist to respond. Children like these games because they allow their preferred mode of play; therapists like them because they allow their preferred mode of work. Therapists are eager to hear about their patients and seek opportunities to offer interpretations or suggestions, and these therapeutically directive games offer this information and opportunities within the context of an otherwise typical board game.

Therapeutic games include those made up individually by therapists for and with their child patients and those that have been published. Published games are typically those in which activities focus on using specific materials like puppets (Blackwell, 1997; Boutlinghouse, 1997; Cook, 1997b; Cunliffe, 1997; Harkin, 1997; Jacobs, 1997; Matisse, 1997; Narcavage, 1997; G. F. Short, 1997b), storytelling (Frederiksen, 1997; Jacobs, 1997), cameras (Cook, 1997a; Tierney, 1997) and such, or on eliciting specific content like anger (Benedict, 1997; Cangelosi, 1997; Davidson, 1997; Glatthorn, 1997; Horn, 1997; Leonetti, 1997; Meagher, 1997; McDowell, 1997; Saxe, 1997; Wunderlich, 1997), experiences of abuse (Saxe, 1997b; Schmidt, 1997; A. H. Short, 1997), or earlier memories of childhood (Agre, 1997a; Brown, 1997; Cook, 1997c; Heidt, 1997; Pitzen, 1997; Schaefer, 1997; G. F. Short, 1997c).

What these games have in common is their attempt to relate the treatment directly to the child's real life. The therapist directs the child's play in order to get the child to express some aspect of current or past life, directly or metaphorically, and the therapist intervenes by discussing the real-life event. Therapists can be understanding or empathetic, accepting or restructuring, all as applied to the real event described in the child's structured play.

## THE TALKING, FEELING, DOING GAME

Probably the best known of these games is the Talking, Feeling, Doing Game (Gardner, 1973), so it will be the primary game used to demonstrate therapeutic techniques here. The game is very typical of structured games: There is a game board, with a path of different colored squares winding from Start to Finish. Players win chips for successful play; the player with the most chips at the end of the game wins. Dice tosses dictate how far along the path each colored playing piece may move. A player may land on spaces prescribing extra moves, loss of moves, or spinning a dial to offer winning or losing chips. So far, this *is* an ordinary game!

The game becomes extraordinary when a player lands on a white, yellow, or pink square and therefore picks a white, yellow, or pink card. These are the talking, feeling, and doing cards respectively, and they ask players to describe or pretend to act out life events or feelings. The assignments range from relatively unemotional, nonanxiety-producing tasks such as "How old are you?"

"What's your favorite color?" and "Clap your hands three times," to highly emotionally charged ones such as "What's the worst thing you can say about your family?" "How do you feel about a girl who touches her private parts in public?" and "Pretend you're having a bad dream and tell what the dream is about." If a player completes the assignment, he or she receives a chip. The game is highly useful therapeutically, then, because the child's motivation to win the game leads her to want more chips, while the therapist's motivation to understand the child leads him to want the child to earn more of these chips. The game provides the structure preferred by latency-age children while encouraging them to express their deepest feelings and rewarding them for doing so.

## USE OF THE THERAPIST'S TURN

A noteworthy feature of these therapeutic games is that both the child and the therapist are expected to respond to expressive tasks. While the child is developing the ability to trust the therapist and openly express herself, she is also learning about the therapeutic process and about the therapist. The therapist playing along with a child patient also picks a card or piece of paper or toy object when it is his turn and is expected to describe or play out some aspect of his own life or fantasies. This is a sensible concept: The therapist is modeling the expressive process for the child and is offering himself as a partner in the exploration of thoughts and feelings. In reality, however, many therapists feel uncomfortable about the idea of exposing too much of themselves to their young patients. The "therapeutic" in the game is supposed to be for the child, not the therapist! Some therapists admit that they own the game but do not display it in the therapy room out of concern over how to answer revealing questions when they play with their patients.

Most writers have dealt with this dilemma by describing how to tailor their own responses to instruct the child in more appropriate behavior in the world or to teach some moral lesson about life. Richard Gardner (1973, 1983) recommends that the therapist try to enhance the child's competence or reduce the child's anger by setting examples and providing illustrations of optimum functioning. For example, in answer to the question "What sport are you worst at?" Gardner (1983) proposes replying, "I'm so poor at so many . . . I'm particularly bad at basketball . . . I know that if I practiced more, I could be better" (p. 265).

This, Gardner claims, gives the child an understanding that the therapist is "a human being with liabilities of his or her own" (p. 265) as well as identifies the solution for the therapist's—and, implicitly, for the patient's—problems as practice and hard work.

The game can be used in a slightly different way if the therapist sees the game as an opportunity to provide interpretations and enhance expressiveness rather than to provide solutions to problems. Most children in therapy have often had the experience of trying as hard as they could but still failing, or of feeling that no amount of hard work could possibly make a dent in their problems. Suggesting a solution of trying harder is unlikely to cause much significant change in them. If the therapist's goal is deeper understanding rather than a rapid solution, the reply might better be one that identifies the dilemma and the frustrations experienced by the child, and by the therapist, too, as a fellow human being—but without resolution or outlet.

In the answer to the question above, then, the therapist might still tailor her response to the child's needs, but without dictating a solution to the problem. She could admit to being poor at basket-ball—or tennis, or swimming, or whatever could be somewhat honestly described—but then continue to discuss the feelings that accompany the liability, rather than the proper solution to the problem. She might go on to talk about being too short—or heavy or weak or even afraid—and about how frustrated she is when she fails, how envious she is of other people's abilities, or how angry she is at herself for not feeling adequate. That way she expresses the problem and the feelings she might have about it, much as a patient might express the problem and the feelings, but she stops before offering any solutions. In this way, the therapist can show the child that he is understood, that his problem is not unique or bizarre, and that therapy is a place to display feelings and work on weaknesses. It opens the door to further discussion and exploration, allowing the child to express his own feelings of inadequacy as well as design his own effective means of overcoming the inadequacies. The child learns that everyone feels deficient at some time, becomes freer to feel and to cope with feeling frustrated, and begins to see therapy as a place to express frustration and possibly explore methods of coping. The therapist is purposely not presented as the more competent one with answers; therapy is presented as a place for the child to explore and develop his own competencies.

## TRUTHFULNESS OF RESPONSES

In both Gardner's (1973, 1975, 1983) method of responding and the one proposed here, the therapist should be aware of the child's needs in responding to his own assignments. It may be useful

(Gardner, 1973, 1983) for the therapist to be self-revelatory to show children that the therapist is fallibly human. However, full disclosure may not be helpful to the child, whose welfare should be the top priority. For example, the "best thing that happened to you today" might honestly be a sexual experience the therapist enjoyed before going to work that day. While describing this would be the most honest way to answer the question, it is probably not in the child's best interest to do so. The therapist could truthfully say, "My family was warm and loving this morning; we got along really well and didn't have any fights and said nice things to each other. It made me feel really good when I left home today."

This scene is one that children can identify with and fantasize about; the response can serve to bring the child and therapist closer together in a shared definition of "best things that can happen," and the treatment can progress further toward helping the child become expressive of likes, dislikes, and wishes.

Therapeutic games, like all board games, address the needs of latency-age children. Children at this age will not talk, so talk therapy is not available; they do not always play dramatically, so interpretation of symbols portrayed there is not always possible. But the material children reveal in answer to game questions can be understood projectively, and the therapist's turn can be used to express interpretations of that material metaphorically.

## EXAMPLES OF POSSIBLE RESPONSES

Let us look at some other cards and possible responses to the cards that might further the goal of exploration and interpretation.

## *Talking Cards*

**What things come into your mind when you can't fall asleep?**

In reality, I may worry about my career, my finances, my family, my aging body, money, a paper I'm supposed to be writing, HMOs, money, whether I'm a good enough mother, whether I'll ever get another referral, money, and so on—and I really can go on sleeplessly all night. However, once again, it is not very useful for my child patient to know the details of all this. It is useful, however, for him to understand that I, too, am sleepless sometimes, that I have worries that keep me awake, and that they can upset me like they upset him. So I might say:

> Well, I worry, generally, about things I'm anxious about the next day, or doing something the next day that I'm scared of, or something. And then, once I can't fall asleep because I'm worried, I start to worry about not falling asleep, and then I can't fall asleep because I'm worried about not falling asleep! And then I start to think that I'll NEVER fall asleep, and that keeps me up even more! And then it gets later and later, and then I worry that it's almost morning but I'm not asleep yet, and that keeps me up even more! I HATE that!

This answer is dramatic and long, but vague. My creating fully developed, expressive answers helps children be able to do the same when it is their turn; I have shown by example that the best answers are those that are descriptive and dramatic—maybe even melodramatic—and highly revealing. I am purposefully vague about the content of my worries, not as an example to be followed, but because the most important issue is what my difficulties are when I am worried, not what the worries are in themselves. This is particularly most important for my treatment with the child, because this is the aspect we share. If I know that a child has a particular worry—separation anxiety, performance fears, noise phobia—I can include something similar in my own response as well if I can truthfully find a connection in my own life:

> I sometimes worry about being alone, that something bad will happen to me and nobody will be there to help me. . . .

> If I have a big day the next day, like sometimes I'm supposed to give a speech to a big group of people who do my same job, I get really worried that I will forget what I'm supposed to say. . . .

> Sometimes if it's dark and really late, I might hear a noise, like a creak or a clunk or something. I know it's just a normal night noise because I live in an old house in a big city. But if it's dark, I sometimes get scared that it might mean somebody's there. . . .

If I cannot find a way to relate my "worries" to the child's—either because I never have even vaguely similar worries or because I cannot think fast enough to come up with one—I can use any generic list of worries, since my hope is simply to communicate the ideas that everyone has worries, that they keep many people awake at night, and that the purpose of therapy is to be able to admit and share these worries.

## What do you say to someone whose foot you stepped on by mistake?

I am probably more socially presentable than most of my child patients, but most of them do know the appropriate behavior in such circumstances, even if they do not always perform it. I could answer, "I say, excuse me, I'm sorry," and move on to the next card, but that would mean a wasted opportunity to explore the child's feelings and experiences—the reason we are there together. So I might more usefully express the commonly occurring conflict between what one is supposed to say and what one feels like saying:

> Well, it depends on whose foot it is. If it's a stranger, like at a movie theater or something, I would probably just say, "Excuse me," like I'm supposed to. But if I know the person I might like them a lot, and then I'd feel really bad and embarrassed that I stepped on them, so I'd say, "Are you okay? I'm really sorry. I didn't mean to do that. It was a mistake. Excuse me, please." Or if I didn't like the person, I might be *glad* to step on them, maybe hard, so I wouldn't want to say anything. Or I'd feel like saying, "Excuuuuuuuuuuuse meeeeee. I'm sooooooo not sorry!"

This kind of comment opens up the possibility of exploring every child's battle with socialization—the desire to do the right thing and the oppositional or aggressive feelings that sometimes conflict with that desire. At the very least, it suggests that I understand that many people have these kinds of conflicts, and I am ready to listen to the child's expression of them if he is ever interested in sharing them with me, either in play or in discussion. Adam stopped me as

I finished my first sentence: "It depends on whose foot it is. . . ." He interrupted to ask, "What if it was the president of the United States?"

His question was informative in several ways. First, it dramatized how very anxious this boy is about the power of authorities and his fear of retaliation; there are no small errors in his world, no small offenses. He doesn't imagine stepping on the kid next door, only the foot of the Leader of the Free World! Second, it showed me how absorbed in the game he was, that he interrupted exuberantly to be sure I addressed his questions directly. Third, it showed me that he understood the purpose of the game and was participating fully. Adam recognized that I was there to try to understand exactly what worried him and to help him tolerate and overcome his anxieties. In describing exactly what his anxieties are—in the metaphor of the game, in the example of the president—he helped me to help him. I answered:

Well, if it really was the president of the United States, I'd feel really terribly awful. Yipes! I'd really really apologize about 12 times, and I'd probably feel bad for the whole rest of the day. I'd be so excited to see the president that I'd want to make a good impression, and here I went and stepped on his foot. Ugh. . . .

And we could share a moment of understanding about what it feels like to feel embarrassed, to want to make a good impression and be unable to, to feel foolish for a very long time over a small mistake, and to worry about Grand Authorities. This can allow me to show him that I am interested in such feelings; in fact, Adam has begun to try to tell me about his real anxieties for a few minutes at the beginning of each session, sitting and talking for as long as he can tolerate the discomfort. I believe his ability to talk to me about difficult topics grew from my describing experiences like the one above during our game play.

## Feeling Cards

**How do you feel about someone who's the teacher's pet?**

It is important to consider the underlying question posed by the card. This one is not about my true experiences with teachers' pets, but seems to wonder about feelings evoked by observation of other people: What does it feel like when someone else is favored by an authority, and what does it feel like when someone else's behavior is more exemplary than one's own? The former question might apply more to a child with intense sibling rivalry, and might suggest a therapist answer like:

> It makes me angry. I want the teacher to pay attention to *me*, not to somebody else. I don't think it's fair for a teacher to like one person in the class better than the others, and I don't think it's right for them to show it if they do. Everybody in the class needs help and attention, and it feels bad to me if somebody else gets more than I do.

The latter question might apply more to a child who has a history of disobedience or acting out in class, and who might respond better to an answer such as:

I *hate* that. Just because one kid might know the answers better doesn't mean they get to have the teacher's attention more. Really, it's the kids who don't know the right answer that the teacher should pay attention to more. The goody-goodies in the class just make me mad.

These answers are tailored to the needs of two different categories of children, with two different primary concerns. They are loosely descriptive of the therapist's life—because they are descriptive of conflicts in everyone's life—and designed to evoke an experience of my sharing the child's feelings. They are descriptive of some of the many feelings I actually experience, but chosen because they might speak to the specific child I have in front of me during this game.

In addition, the answers are truly "feeling" answers, with no solution implied. If anything, they might be heard by some as overly supportive of the child's inappropriate behaviors. In practice, however, children rarely hear these answers that way; they usually respond with admiration that I seem to understand their feelings in these situations (they've even offered me *two* chips for my response!), and they often bring up their own real experiences with siblings or classmates who are more favored or better behaved. So the talk therapy is enhanced, and real-life solutions are opened for consideration by my leaving my own solution unstated.

**Tell about a time when your feelings were hurt.**

To tailor this response to a particular patient, one needs to ask oneself what hurts that child's feelings. Is this a child who is teased by classmates? Is the last one picked for sports teams? Is embarrassed by an inability to read? Has been moved from foster home to foster home? Is ignored at home because a sibling is favored? Is torn apart by parental arguments? While no therapist lives through these difficulties daily and most will never have had these experiences, everyone has been teased, embarrassed, ignored, concerned. These can be described in general terms in a way that expresses universal human experiences that children can identify with:

Once, I really didn't understand what I was supposed to: a friend was trying to explain something in the newspaper to me, and I just didn't get it. My friend was not nice about it—he got really nasty and told me I wasn't trying hard enough or I must be really stupid. And that really hurt my feelings, because I'm *not* stupid and I *was* trying, but I just didn't get it. When he talked to me that way it hurt my feelings.

Once I had a lunch date with a friend, and I really wanted to go to lunch with her because I had something I wanted to talk to her about—I wanted her help me with a decision I had to make. But when it got to be time for lunch she told me she couldn't go because she was going to have lunch with somebody else. I was really hurt, and really mad, because that wasn't fair for her to pick somebody else when she already promised me.

I have two friends that I like a lot, but they really don't like each other at all. So whenever I see them, I have to be sure I only see one of them at a time, and I can't even invite both of them to my parties. And sometimes they even tell me bad things about the other one. That really hurts because I like them both, but it's hard to like them when I hear bad things about them all the time.

These answers express the kinds of feelings children often experience, with some degree of honesty about the kinds of experiences therapists have had; they all represent a version of some experience that did happen to me during the preparation of this chapter. They usually lead children to feel understood, accepted, and similar to the therapist; they often help children express the experiences of hurt feelings they have had in their own lives so that these experiences are available for discussion in treatment.

**What part of your body do you like the least? Why?**

This question sounds like it calls for the therapist to reveal highly personal information; it is the kind of card that makes many child therapists turn red, stammer a quick answer, and later hide the game from future use. But it need not. Once again, a consideration of what the card is exploring and how it might relate to children can point the way to an answer that is useful to the child and not threatening to the therapist.

What do children like least about themselves? Usually young children do not yet pay a great deal of attention to their physical bodies, so the most hated aspect of themselves is likely to be a life experience or the lack of a skill. Children hate being abandoned to foster care, being badly treated by abusive parents, living with arguing or divorced parents, having to wear glasses, and/or being unable to read or write well. They typically feel these are the result of some failing of their own and that they imply underlying unacceptability or a fatal flaw in their character, and that there is no hope for them. With this in mind, a therapist can honestly choose any body part to describe, mention it briefly, and continue with a discussion of the evoked feeling that might be shared with the child:

47

I never liked my bottom, because it always seemed too big for my body. And I feel like people look at me and think, "Ooh, she's really fat and ugly," and then they decide they don't like me just because they don't like my butt, and they don't even give me a chance to get to know them.

I hate the way my voice gets all high and squeaky when I get nervous. So I get all worried that everybody is listening to me and thinking that I'm really goofy. So I get so nervous when there are people around that my voice starts to get squeaky. So I don't say anything so nobody will notice my yucky voice. But then I end up wishing I *could* talk, because I'd like to have more friends, but I'm embarrassed.

I don't like being so short, and I don't like that I can't do anything about how tall I am. Even though I didn't decide to be short, and there's no way I could change it no matter what I do, it feels like maybe if I was different, or if I had been different when I was little—like if I drank more milk or ate more vegetables or got more exercise or something—maybe I could've changed that. I *know* I couldn't, but it makes me feel bad anyway.

These answers deal with "hated parts" of the therapist, briefly, but concentrate much more on the emotional content of having a hated part of the self—a common experience—so that children can relate and explore their own feelings rather than attend to the exposure of the therapist. Sometimes this leads children to immediately share their similar experiences: "Kids don't give me a chance either"; "I wish I could have more friends, too"; "I sometimes wish I could disappear like that"; "I feel like everything is my fault sometimes, too." In any event, they feel that I am someone who can be trusted to understand feelings, whether they tell me directly in words or show me in their play.

### *Doing Cards*

**Show what you would do if you were turned into your mother.**

This card, when picked by a child, is highly revealing. We would see a child play out some aspect of his mother—mom's anger or disgust or obsession with cleaning or preoccupation with work. In addition, we would be able to discover something about the child's reactions to his mother—he would be happy to become his mother or dismayed, he would be just like his mother or try to be entirely different. It therefore seems highly revealing when picked by a therapist.

Once again, though, it need not be. If we speak to the child patient in our answer, our relationships with our own mothers become irrelevant. My preference here is to begin my answer at a point close to what I imagine is the child's experience of her mother and then raise an experience which might be farther from consciousness. For a child who is aware of adoring her mother but not of her mother's flaws, I might say:

> I'd be really glad to be my mother because my mother is a really good cook, so if I turned into her I could cook good stuff all the time. But I'd also try to be a little better at the things she's not so good at—like when she's in the middle of cooking she

doesn't pay any attention to anything but what she's cooking. So I would try to cook but still pay attention to my children when they needed me.

And then I would pretend to cook something good like chocolate chip cookies, and could pretend to refuse to pay attention to an imaginary child at the same time.

For a child aware of her rage but not her mother's strengths, I might offer:

If I turned into my mother I would hate it unless I got to become her and then be different from her. Like my mother yells a lot, and I really wouldn't like to be like that. But she's a great story reader. So if I could turn into my mother but I could read good stories and be able to stop yelling so much, then it would be okay.

And then I could pretend to read a story to my imaginary child but pretend to stop myself from yelling.

**You're sitting on the beach and a bottle with a piece of paper in it washes up on the shore. You take the paper out of the bottle. What does it say?**

This card actually might be asking a number of questions. First, it calls for some amount of empathy, since it is about reading a message in a bottle, not writing one (there is also a card about writing one). The classic Message in a Bottle is one about someone abandoned on a desert island, with no food or water or means of escape. A recent book and movie about a message in a bottle was about someone pining for love rather than safety. Internet chat rooms offer their own venues for messages sent out to anonymous strangers in hopes of finding something not available at home.

The question for the therapist is which message might speak to the needs of the child before her. Does he most wish for love, safety, freedom, escape, reliability, skill? How could the message in this imaginary bottle express that?

It says, "Please help me. I am at 229 West 71st Street, and I am a good, nice, and cooperative person. But all the people who live here with me are mean and nasty, and I need somebody better to take care of me."

It says, "I just got the greatest news and I need to share it with anybody and everybody: I *passed my math test!* I'm so happy I just want to shout it out! Be glad for me, everyone!"

It says, "I'm writing because I don't have anybody else to talk to. I have lots of feelings all bottled up inside, but nobody understands me. I wish I had a real person who could listen to me and know me and still like me anyway for who I really am."

It says, "I just ran away from home because nobody there loves me. I need a new home where everybody would be nice to each other and not argue all the time. Anybody who knows about a home like that, please let me know."

These hypothetical messages all describe a situation potentially familiar to all children, and possibly applicable to the specific child in this therapy playing this game. My answer tells the child that I know something about children—indeed, I may even understand *this* child in some way—that I am available to listen to his wishes, needs, fears, joys and sadness. I have not confronted him directly; that is, I have not suggested that *he* is lonely or scared or unhappy, just that I know that some children sometimes are. I may even have reassured him that he is not the only person in the world to have the feelings he does. In any case, I have laid the groundwork for him to communicate to me further, both in the game and outside, and thus helped move the therapeutic process along.

Thus, the Talking, Feeling, Doing Game can be used in many ways to give children a message about our understanding of their lives and needs and wishes and worries, and about the way therapy can be useful to them in working out their difficulties.

## OTHER THERAPEUTIC GAMES

There are many other games designed for therapeutic purposes, including those mentioned at the beginning of this chapter and others. All can be used in the ways described here, to elicit the child's experiences and feelings, and to offer the therapist's attempts at understanding and interpretation.

In the Bag of Things game (Gardner, 1975), for instance, players pick an object or sometimes a picture of an object out of a bag and make up a story about the object. Stories can be understood as projective material, in which the child's fantasies are expressed symbolically in the story told. Each child tells a story expressing her own particular wishes and needs at that moment in the treatment. For instance, a baby bottle can inspire a story about milk and nurturance in a child feeling full, one about lack of milk and empty larders in a child feeling needy, one about too many babies crying in a child with sibling rivalry, one about withholding milk in an angry child. Therapists, too, can create stories about these themes to interpret these issues to their patients.

### *Therapeutic Use of Therapeutic Games*

These games can all be used to communicate metaphorically with the child in treatment. To the child who tells a story about empty larders, I can say that I understand it must feel really scary to think that there isn't enough and you might not get any. For those with too many babies, I can say that I know how unfair it is that other people get what you might want yourself, that babies get more than older people, that everybody who wants can't have. For those withholding in anger, I can describe the feeling of being so angry that you don't want anybody to have anything and that it might feel good to be able to say, "No!" to someone when you feel that bad yourself.

When I make these comments, I am thinking about the child's real life, full of inadequate supplies of food or love, of other children claiming all the attention, of overwhelming vengeful anger. I don't mention these thoughts directly; I try to make my comments generally applicable to both the game and real life. So I talk about there not being enough to go around, meaning both milk in the story and love in the child's home. I say it feels good to say, "No!" meaning both in the story and in the world.

I then watch for the child's response. Does she want to talk more about the story? We can continue to imagine an empty bottle or fantasize together about how nice it would be if we had zillions of bottles of all the milk in the world.

Does he want to apply it to life? We can talk about the time at school when the cafeteria ran out of milk (or juice or peanut butter or chocolate chip cookies) and he didn't get any, or the time when his mother helped his brother with his homework and his sister with her music lessons but had no time for him, or imagine a world where all you had to do was wish—not three wishes but a zillion wishes—and you could have anything and everything.

Does she want to move quickly on to the next card or object? We can play the game further, while I note that my comments might have been too difficult for her to process at this time, and I try to keep her reaction in mind for use in my next answer in the game.

## THERAPEUTIC GAMES VS. ORDINARY BOARD GAMES

This chapter has described various specially designed therapeutic games and their use in child psychotherapy. The methods described here can be applied to any of these therapeutic games, including the Talking, Feeling, Doing Game, other published therapeutic games, and games created by therapists for use in their own offices with the children they see in treatment.

Therapeutic board games offer the opportunity for latency-age children to play the structured games they prefer, in their developmental stage between the dramatic play of the younger years and the talk therapy of adolescence and beyond, while helping therapists discover more about their lives outside treatment.

But finding out about the child's life is not therapy. Taking a psychosocial history, through games or otherwise, allows us to begin treatment, and it can be helpful in understanding the past development of current difficulties, but it does not constitute the treatment itself. Playing these specially designed therapeutic games has the same purpose: It brings the child's life issues into the playroom so that they can be discussed therapeutically. But latency-age children are not discussers; even after you know they had a fight in school last week, they are not interested in talking to you about how it started and what it felt like and how it got resolved.

There is another potential drawback to therapeutic games: It may be easier to misinterpret the play of the child:

Freddie had been playing the Talking, Feeling, Doing Game for several consecutive weeks in all therapy sessions. He preferred landing on "spin" squares and often made certain that he did. When he experienced a run of losses from the spinner, however, he began to take his chances on colored squares. Answering was clearly difficult for him, a fact that I noticed and mentioned at times. Some of the questions stirred up so much anxiety that he was visibly disturbed, beginning to fidget and wriggle in his chair as he played. Regularly, he would reach a point where it seemed he could not bear the rising internal pressure; he would throw the board across the room, scattering all pieces and chips and ending our play for the day. I understood this to be a response to anxiety raised by the questions he was answering, becoming unbearable due to the content of the most recent card picked. But saying so had no effect. I repeatedly suggested, "That was a hard one" and "It's really hard to talk about that kind of thing" and "It's too hard to even *think* about that one" . . . to no avail. Week after week as we played the game, Freddie became more and more agitated and threw the game off the table, regardless of what I tried to understand and discuss.

Finally, after many sessions like this, Freddie took out a different game, one involving no therapeutic questions at all, just throwing the dice, moving around the board, and winning or spending money. I assumed he was avoiding the anxiety of the Talking, Feeling and Doing questions, and said so. Without response. We played the Money Game for a while, until Freddie began to fidget and wriggle, just as he had before in our play. Eventually, he threw this board across the room as well, scattering dollars and coins and playing pieces everywhere. Now I was confronted with the real issue: It was the play that caused his anxiety, not the content of the cards he was faced with. True, Freddie threw the game across the room when he became frustrated, but what was frustrating to him was not the particular questions asked each time but his failure to succeed at the game. He was upset that I moved ahead of him, that I had more money than he did, that I might be winning.

There was something—his worries about failure—in this structured experience within the treatment that he was struggling with; it had nothing to do with what he had expressed about his outside life. I had been lulled into thinking I understood him because he had been giving me lots of information about his thoughts and feelings. On the contrary, I could not understand him until he stopped telling me about his life and forced me to look at his behavior in the structured board game without looking at his life events at all.

In this case, playing a game to find out about the issues in Freddie's real life served to move us away from the real issues of his life. He needed to show me that he was frustrated over losing and worried about failing and the resulting terrible damage to his self-esteem; these were the real issues he faced in life. The therapeutic game allowed him to show me these feelings, but I was so involved in the content of his responses—the information he seemed to be telling me about his life—that I failed to look at the process of his responses. Knowing the details of Freddie's life took me away from the therapeutic process; finding meaning in his use of the structure of a board game allowed me to help him more.

# CHAPTER FOUR

# Cheaters Never Lose

Tessa wants to play Chutes and Ladders, and *only* Chutes and Ladders. She spins to see who goes first and wins the spin. She spins again for her turn, counts her four squares, and hands me the spinner. We play like this—spin, count, spin, count, spin, count—until she reaches the last square. She then continues—spin, count, spin, count—from the beginning while I continue on my first lap. And so on until the end of the session.

This is indeed an apparently nontherapeutic use of board games. Other than Tessa's insistence that we play this game only and that we keep playing this game, there is no obvious emotional content, no clear symbolic expression, no evident psychodynamics displayed. It is a structured game played in a structured way, yielding little obvious information about the child in treatment. It seems to be an illustration of the way the game is supposed to be played, and as such seems to be a detriment rather than an enhancement to the therapeutic process. We certainly would not want to encourage children in therapy to use therapy time in this way; it seems to support the argument that so many previous writers have put forth that structured games should be kept out of the playroom.

I think these writers have missed the usefulness of board games because of their focus on this kind of fair play. Writers have discussed their attempts to keep the child playing fairly and to stop what they call cheating. In one of the few early articles to date written specifically about cheating, John Meeks (1970) described children's needs to cheat because of their difficulty accepting the externally imposed structure of the games and their "inability to accept losing [a game] without a severe drop in self-esteem" (p. 158). He suggested that children have conflicts about cheating and that these conflicts are externalized when the child cheats and the adult confronts the child about it. Accordingly, he suggested that this cheating be allowed to unfold in treatment, then be questioned. Other authors (e.g., Beiser, 1970) suggest stopping the cheating quickly. Only recently (Bellinson, 2000; Herman, 2000; Krimendahl, 2000; Meeks, 2000), has there been discussion in the literature of the productive use of children's cheating in therapy.

I think efforts to stop cheating are misguided. In my experience, even the most egregious cheaters know what the rules of the game are, that they are breaking them, and that this is not permissible in the real world. They already have their parents, teachers, peers, and siblings to teach them the reality principle; they do not need their psychotherapists for that. In addition, to paraphrase Tolstoy (Anna Karenina, Part 1, Chapter 1), all fair players resemble one another; every cheater cheats in his or her own fashion. Box-top rules require the same kind of play from every player in every game, and therapists who insist on following these rules are doomed to repeated battles over the rules with their patients. And if they succeed, the result is a boring, repetitious game with little therapeutic value, like Tessa's play.

I noticed this with Ted, a very bright, obsessional 6-year-old boy who wanted to play War with me. (Here again, the choice of games is instructive in itself. So many of them are designed and named to replicate life's struggles: War, Sorry, Headache, Spit. . . .) When I asked whether he was looking at his cards before putting them down, Ted said, "No, I like to play by the rules." I thought to myself "No! Save me! *This* is what therapists mean when they talk about how boring board games are!"

Fortunately, he soon changed the game to be one more expressive of his emotions—smashing his hands onto my cards when he captured them, throwing cards across the room when I captured them, picking the ace of clubs to put down on every round. At last we had some interesting dynamics to work with!

It seems clear from these two examples that, at the very least, fair play leads to therapeutically unproductive time, and more useful playtime requires more expressive use of the materials.

Consider the ways other playroom materials are used. One would never tell a child how those had to be used: "Don't put the toilet in the bedroom, it has to be in the bathroom"; "You can't draw an elephant today, you have to draw a dinosaur"; "You have to choose either a revolver or a laser gun, you can't have one in each hand"; "The soldiers have to be used on the battlefield, they can't come into the dollhouse." These statements seem ridiculous. Perhaps we feel justified in controlling our patients' use of structured games because proper play with them involves following rules. But we are not trying to use them properly; we are trying to use them therapeutically. They should be part of the process of treatment. When children use toys or dolls or art supplies or other playroom materials, therapists watch to see what is created, used, and revealed in the play. Structured games, too, can be highly informative if they are seen as projective material—regardless of what the box top says or how they are used in other contexts.

## UNDERSTANDING RULE BREAKING

Game play usually starts, for most latency-age children if not for Claire in Chapter 2, with proper play according to the rules. Children sometimes ask or demand or beg to go first rather than tossing the dice for that, or to have the therapist shuffle and deal, or to be allowed to be Red or Professor Plum or Banker. Then they play. Properly. Boringly.

Even this play, though, can reveal some amount of dynamics if we are prepared to notice and interpret. Tessa, for example, insists on one particular game; perhaps this is a sign of her strong determination or even stubbornness in other contexts. The game she picks is one that requires only simple counting—no reading, deducing, or strategizing, in spite of her ability by age and intelligence to use these skills. She then insists that we play, play, play—spinning quickly, counting immediately, alternating turns rapidly. This, too, is an indication of her psychodynamics; she is a child who is upset and embarrassed by her emotions. She represses them until they burst out in tears or rage. She denies them; she tells me she wants me not to mention them, to her or to anyone else. Even in playing by the box-top rules, then, Tessa reveals dynamic information about her emotions and character.

I can help Tessa even while playing a simple board game according to box-top rules because she does reveal herself in the game. She insists we play, play, play. I tell her I notice that she wants to concentrate on the game and that she wants me not to talk about anything. I suggest that the other things on her mind must be very frightening to her, for her to want to play so hard and so fast. I mention that if we play like this the whole time, without talking or resting, she can be sure that I will never have a chance to bring up all those other things on her mind—like her difficulties at school or her arguing and divorcing parents. I can also describe the way this is like the rest of her life, where she wants to forget that these difficulties exist and feels she can if only she tries hard to never think of them, but that this way her difficulties never seem to really go away, and she never seems to gain any help in dealing with them. In talking with Tessa this way I am describing what I notice about her personality—in the board game and also in her life—and the way in which her defensive style leads to further difficulties for her. We can talk about them or play about them, either in real life (by discussing what she's afraid might happen to her if she thinks about her parents' divorce) or in the game (by seeing what it feels like to slow up the game to the point that we can think about what we are doing). So even proper box-top play, within official rule structure, can allow some amount of therapeutic work to occur. Creative play (cheating) allows even more.

When and how children begin to stretch the rules reveals

additional important information about their dynamics. Some children start immediately, some begin after some minor frustration— the therapist being ahead on the game board or making a match successfully—some only when they are in imminent danger of losing the game. This reveals information about their frustration tolerance, their ability to delay gratification, and the circumstances in which they feel threatened.

## STYLES OF RULE BREAKING

How they stretch the rules is also of interest. Some children peek at other players' cards or the solution cards. Some deal themselves from other than the top of the deck. Some throw the dice over and over until the "right" number comes up, some physically move the dice to put them where they want them. Some try to hide what they are doing. Some try to pretend there was some sort of mistake, some do it blatantly. Some "confess" after they have cheated for a while.

Tessa enters the session and takes out Chutes and Ladders— only Chutes and Ladders—as she had at our previous session. She spins to see who goes first, but doesn't seem to like the number she gets. She declares it "on the line" and spins again, getting a winning number this time. She chooses her playing piece. The first square is Number 1, containing a ladder up the board to Number 38. Tessa puts her piece on Number 1 while she spins her turn, but since she is sitting on a ladder, she moves up it immediately, then counts the rest of her turn. She invites me to begin similarly, up the first ladder.

Ian plays Trouble, trying to move around the board as quickly as possible. He pops the die and gets a one, announces that the one was mine from last turn—he hasn't yet popped—and pops again for a higher number.

Vinny chooses Uno, and we play a long, fair game according to box-top rules. He comes close to winning once; I come close to winning once. We go through the deck twice. I have "Uno," then by sheer luck am able to go out after his next card. He hands my last card back to me, takes back his last move, and replaces it with a card I cannot match. I pick until I can play on his card, and he wins within three more moves.

Harvey plays Mastermind. He is the "master," I the "mind," trying to guess his code. It is hard for him to wait for me to think or to guess incorrectly; he tells me which of my guesses is correct and which is not. Then I create a code, and he guesses. He is surprisingly good, making what seem to be very lucky guesses very quickly and cracking the code accurately within four or five trials. As he leaves the office at the end of the session he says, "You know, you can cheat at that game really easy." "Did you cheat?" I ask. "Yes," he says, "I looked while you were making up your pattern." And he walks out the door.

Tessa surreptitiously takes what she wants, assuming she will be permitted to do so. She announces her second spin and which square she can begin on. She is comfortable sharing her good fortune with me as long as she can have it for herself. Ian lies to get what he wants. Vinny blatantly reverses time in his "do-over." Harvey is so guilty over his behavior that he confesses. These patterns match these children's character styles in the rest of their lives as well: Tessa is a doted-on only child who insists on being given whatever she wants but has plenty and so can share easily. Ian makes up his own rules in his refusal to follow those imposed on him. Vinny openly demands that his family stop talking about anything upsetting, as if it never happened. Harvey is a silent, guilty child who punishes himself severely whenever anyone criticizes him. Thus, these vignettes of children cheating demonstrates the aspects of their personality that brought them into treatment.

How long children go on cheating is relevant as well. Some, once they have started, continue to the end of the game or the session. Some cheat just long enough to get ahead, then play within the rules until they experience the need again.

> Benji is playing Sorry. He has two pieces in "Home" to my one—a lead, but not a sure win. He throws a three. He is one square behind a green "Slide"; I am two squares in front of it. He has played according to box-top rules for most of this game but seems unable to resist this. He counts "one," slides to the other end of the green slide, then "two, three," and sends me back home. He continues the game, sliding across every Slide he crosses, whether he lands on it or not. (Box-top rules require sliding only when landing at the beginning of the Slide by exact count, only on a Slide of a color other than one's own.) He beats me handily. Next session he begins Sorry again, playing by box-top rules to start, then beginning extra Slides as the game goes on.

Benji is able to follow Sorry rules for limited periods of time. Once he begins to cheat he is unable to stop for the rest of the session.

Similarly in his life, he is able to follow rules, at home and at school, but after a while he refuses to do what he is asked and cannot become cooperative again until a major argument has left authorities yelling at him in rage or punishing him.

Some children push themselves just far enough ahead to win; some need to be far, far in the lead. Some (Loomis, 1964) even cheat so as *not* to win the game.

Carl played Candyland, searching out cards early in the game to send himself to the last leg of the journey, then waiting there, inching his way forward until the therapist caught up, then sent himself just barely ahead again to win by a hair.

Adena played Monopoly. She has monopolies and hotels on much of the property on the board. I also have holdings, but I have been less lucky in my throws so I have very little cash. I land on Tennessee Avenue, with a hotel, requiring me to pay her $950. She insists that I pay her only $900 since that is all the cash I have. On my next turn I have received some income from her paying me on her turn, but it is not enough for the $1,100 I owe her for Illinois Avenue rent. She wants me to skip the turn, not to pay her, to pay her from the bank rather than from my own assets.

All these styles of bending and stretching rules, as most styles of playing, can be understood, then interpreted, as indications of the children's dynamics. Because these behaviors are transferential, they can be seen as windows into the lives and the object relations the children experience in their families. Children who cheat early in the game tend to be needier in general than children with the ego strength to wait longer. Children who cannot win may be demonstrating some conflict over the competitive or Oedipal struggles they experience at home. Children who coyly ask for special privileges and favors show the regressive or seductive style they have acquired in response to their environment.

Box-top rules require standardized structured play from every player during every game and therefore may stifle therapeutic productivity. They allow a game to occur while therapy takes place in a verbal realm—much like an adolescent might use a game for respite from potentially painful talk therapy—but they do not allow the game itself to provide much psychological information. Creative play, on the other hand—that is, bending box-top rules or doing what might in other contexts be called cheating—can be as expressive and symbolically revealing as any other playroom play. In this way, a child can develop the use of structured games that is expectable and desirable at the age of latency while continuing the therapeutic process. The therapist can be both an interpreter of dynamics and a guide to a more mature use of board games.

Many therapists are uncomfortable letting children "get away with" cheating, and this leads these therapists to feel uneasy playing with children in this way. If cheating can be relabeled as creative play and seen as symbolic or expressive play, it may free therapists to play with children more comfortably. Therapists can then watch for and interpret children's behavior as expressed in this creative play. Sessions are then therapeutically productive, and therapists can feel satisfied with their work. Discomforts that arise after this can be understood as emerging from the therapeutic alliance and can be interpreted as such. These discomforts are discussed further in Chapter 8.

## CHILDREN WHO DO NOT CHEAT

Are there some children who do not cheat?

I am observing children in their school setting. I attend a session of free time, where four 9- and 10-year-olds are playing Sorry. They play well and fairly for many minutes. Billy is stuck at Start. The others have two and even three pieces in Home, but Billy cannot draw the 1 or 2 card he needs to start the game. He is calm about it, and accepting. There is good-natured teasing of Billy's terrible luck; the others ask if he was a bad boy today, if he is being punished for something, if he is under some sort of curse. They suggest they just skip his turn, because he'll never get anywhere anyway. They even offer him a break: He can start a piece for free, or they will trade him their 1 card for his 7 card. Billy laughs them off, calmly drawing one high number after another. It is never clear whether he will have even started before someone else has won.

The other three, meanwhile, play on. Sonya, Debbie, and Zach are closely matched, each doing well. They "Sorry" each other freely and playfully. Zach and Debbie have three pieces in Home, Sonya two. Zach "Sorry's" Debbie, sending her closest-to-winning piece back to Start. This leaves him in the lead but with his last piece just beginning. He miscounts, claiming to land on a slide space. The group yells. He moves back, and there is an argument over which square he began on—he disputes the position the other three agree on. They insist, and he acquiesces. Again, Zach miscounts and argues. He gets angrier and more insistent at each turn, as he claims to have landed on slides or other players' spaces, or he contests the rules, demanding that the group prove their position. He demurs only when a teacher threatens to remove him from the game.

This is a striking example of children's needs or lack of need to cheat. Zach was the only child in this group who was in therapy. The other three were struggling with the socialization requirements of latency more successfully, both in the game and in their lives. Billy, in particular, seems to have a strong sense of fair play and enough ego strength to be able to tolerate frustration—or even losing in a shut-out—without damage to his self-esteem.

It is not irrelevant, though, that Billy is not in therapy. Children in treatment tend to have far less ego strength, so it is unlikely that a therapist would see that kind of game play in her office. Nevertheless, he is important to keep in our minds, since most children are not in treatment, and his is the kind of functioning we are hoping our child patients will accomplish after successful therapy.

What about children who are in treatment but who do not cheat? There are some children who can play a game according to official rules while talking about other issues—essentially conducting talk therapy while a board game also occurs. This is our goal for life and for treatment, and is the mark of a child who has accomplished a successful latency. So children who do not cheat but who do express their feelings and issues verbally during the game are demonstrating an advanced developmental level.

In my experience, there are very few of these children in treatment before adolescence. Other than achievement of this advanced developmental level, I know of three reasons for children to play in therapy without cheating: fear of the therapist, therapist misunderstanding, or character disorder.

## REASONS FOR NOT CHEATING

Most children old enough to understand the rules begin by using them. Even Zach played according to box-top rules through the start of the game. Then they test the waters and watch for reactions, just as they test limits in other modalities, like turning the lights out, refusing to leave the session, demanding to take toys home. Zach miscounted, then responded to the group's challenge of his count. Children in treatment do this as well, testing for the therapist's response to their miscount. Therapists who insist on rules—consciously or unconsciously—have children who play by the rules, or at least become successful at hiding their breaches. When therapists begin to wonder about creative game play, their child patients often begin to play more creatively. This is described further in Chapter 8.

Second, many therapists misunderstand either the child's play or the box-top rules. I think it is important for therapists to read and understand the published rules for the games in their offices. When a child claims that the rules allow moving backward or jumping two pieces at a time, the therapist should know (as I believe the child does as well) that the box-top rules do not allow this, only the child's rules and wishes do. The therapist can be more useful to the child if she knows what the rules are and watches when and how the child breaks them.

Children sometimes create their own rules and then do not stray from them:

71

Kevin, age 5, plays Sorry. He announces that he will use all the game's rules, plus "my rules." These include moving Sorry cards to the middle and bottom of the deck—sometimes every time they are picked, "Sorry"ing a player only from the square behind—or in front or two spaces away from—the player; starting on 1, 2, 11, or 12 (because 11 and 12 have 1s and 2s in them). He cannot yet read, so he does not know the fine print of backward moves or split or exchange moves.

Melissa—12 years old—plays Uno, every session all session. She plays strictly but using "piles." This means that one can play all one's green cards on a green card, all one's 2s on a 2 card, and so on. She wonders whether a plain Wild Card is the same as or different from a Draw Four Wild Card.

Both of these are creative play, drastically altering the game from the official method of play. Melissa comes close to creating her own new game and playing that game without "cheating." However, it is still creative play and not box-top play. Claiming that Melissa does not cheat is, I think, a misunderstanding. At 12, she certainly can read the game rules, and she is likely to know them from having played in other contexts. For the therapist to ignore her alterations is to miss an opportunity for interpretation and communication with her. And since Melissa plays throughout every session, this is an important opportunity.

Third, there are children in therapy who do not cheat because of a character disorder. I say disorder because I think that for the most part preadolescents in therapy do not have the ego strength—at least not consistently—to adhere to external rules of play. Children in treatment may be able to play some games strictly, or the beginning of every game strictly. But the facts that they are in treatment because they are having some difficulty in their lives, and that they are interested in structured games, usually mean that they are struggling with the way the world imposes rules and expectations on them. And they demonstrate that struggle in their game play.

Children who do not struggle with rules may be regressed—not having begun the struggle, like young children engaged in dramatic play—or they may be suppressed—holding tightly to the world of rules at the expense of spontaneity:

Ted, described above in a game of War, likes "to play by the rules." When he chooses a structured game, he generally does follow box-top rules strictly. He may play forcefully or sloppily, but his play is "official." He does not like games, though. He chooses them in my office one by one, plays until he knows the rules and succeeds at understanding the play, then abandons each game forever. He does not enjoy playing, and in fact gets very little pleasure from anything in his life. My playful spirit only seems to confuse him. He criticizes me for not understanding that it is a board game and for getting overly involved in the play or imagining more metaphoric meaning than is meant to be there.

With Ted, my goal was to accomplish cheating! He did not enjoy his life when he began treatment, had few friends, and did not participate in after-school activities because he could not play. He did invent games to "play" with his classmates, but his classmates complained when Ted insisted on using real money and real outcomes and demanded to continue beyond the point when they wanted to move on to a different game.

> Almost 2 years into the treatment, Ted discovered the game of Life. He was intrigued, as he often was at his discovery of a new game, and particularly interested in this complex game with elaborate rules. He asked many questions about the rules, read all the cards, and found a copy of the game between sessions so he could read the rule book as homework. He played exploratory games through two sessions. In his third session he played again but began to miscount his squares, respin for better numbers, and move me to the squares he preferred me on. The fourth time, he assigned me the lowest salary and himself the highest, chose the best house (and a country house as well!), assigned me the broken one, took enough money to make himself a millionaire, retired quickly to Millionaire Acres, had me banned from his property . . . and then he put the game away and has not opened it since!

This last game was a breakthrough for Ted in his ability to truly play. He turned the game into a fantasy and made all his wishes come true. For Ted, this was not a regressed act but an accomplishment of an earlier stage of development that he had never achieved—possibly one he has to achieve before he can become a successful adult. But it terrified him. His previous strict adherence to rules can be understood in the light of this fear: He had been protecting himself from fantasizing by following the box-top rules.

While this is not the only reason for latency-age children following box-top rules, it is an example of the way in which lack of cheating can be seen as a failure in creative play, open to the same interpretation and therapeutic intervention that the presence of cheating would be. Rule-following play is a strength only when it is accompanied by other signs of maturity, including successful life functioning and the ability to participate in verbal therapy. Otherwise, rule play is probably a sign of the therapist's countertransference or misunderstanding, or of a child's defense against creativity and fun. In any of these cases it should present an opportunity to examine further the dynamics of the therapist and the patient.

## CONCLUSION

Breaking rules is an expectable behavior in children in psychotherapy. Younger children are not yet fully able to follow rules (see Chapter 6), and older children in treatment often do not have the ego strength to play within the boundaries of box-top rules. They may be struggling with the conflict over following or opposing the rules imposed on them by authorities around them, and playing board games, particularly cheating at board games, allows them to work on this issue metaphorically. In addition, rule play is highly structured, routinized, nonrevealing play, while children's creative rulebreaking communicates more information about their dynamics.

When a child takes out a game I ask how we should play, immediately indicating that I have no expectations about rule following. When I find myself in a winning position I ask for the child's preference before making my move, or even help the child prevent me from making it, saying, "If you move there, you leave a double jump for my checkers." Or, "I know the [Clue] answer, should I say it or keep playing?" Or, "I know a lot more [Scrabble] words than you do; should I use just words that you know, too, or should I use harder words that I know but you don't?" Children's responses to these questions are informative: Do they want a fully competitive opponent, or do they prefer special advantages? Do they feel supported by our offers or threatened? Do they need to win by any means necessary, or do they want to try to bring the game to an end fairly? How do they respond when the right card does turn up serendipitously or they land on the square they wanted by luck rather than cheating? Do they want to continue to play for second place, or do they stop when one person wins? Do they respond to the end by starting over? Gloating ecstatically? Throwing game pieces across the room? All these are indications of children's responses to life as well as games, and can be understood and interpreted accordingly.

# CHAPTER FIVE

# The Play's the Thing:
# Finding Meaning in Structured Games

Vinny takes out the game of Life—a game he has played with friends and family and has requested in the playroom. He quickly chooses his car and person, expertly passes out the appropriate amount of money, and properly spins to see who goes first. He follows the college route—slower than moving directly to a career. He follows official rules throughout, with the only exceptions that he looks at all cards when choosing his job and house—rather than taking at random from the decks—and he does not use the one-stock-purchase per player rule. He buys as many stocks as he can whenever he has the money to do so, and he buys car insurance and pays off his college loan on his first payday. He buys home insurance as soon as he acquires a house. He prefers Life cards to almost any other option when given a choice. We play until our time is up, then count our assets to determine the winner.

This represents a typical session with Vinny, a 10-year-old boy who is firmly in the latency stage of development, when he rarely shows interest in dramatic play materials but is drawn to every board game on the shelf. He attempts to discuss his outside life with me but is unable to sustain talk for more than a few moments at a time. He squirms in his seat if I press him to speak, and he left his previous attempt at therapy when that therapist wanted only to talk. He is the sort of child who will attend and enjoy therapy if he is offered structured games to play—and developmentally appropriately so—so that we need to develop ways to help him using his medium.

## FINDING MEANING

Let us look at the game described above to see if there is any meaning that can be understood. On first glance, it may seem to be devoid of psychological meaning: He plays a highly structured version of a highly structured game and plays by the rules most of the time. His ability to use rules this well can be seen as an ego strength, since most children in treatment are not able to sustain this kind of fair play. His choices within even his rule play, and the few places where he changes the rules, do reveal information about his character.

First, his choices: Vinny chooses College and Life cards over Career and money, and he chooses to buy insurance whenever it is available. This suggests that he prefers safe and careful options to instant gratification or more risky behavior. I can use this information to describe his play: "You want to be very careful to take the safest choice"; "You want to be sure you're prepared for anything"; "You'd rather be OK in the end than take something that might be good for now." His rule alterations seem to support this preference: He wants to see all the choices of home design before he chooses one, and he wants to hedge his bets by buying stock in every company.

Is this an accurate portrayal of Vinny's dynamics? Do they appear in his outside life? Before we look to information from outside sources, let's look at other examples of his game-playing style:

At Scrabble:
Vinny plays carefully—he has limited ability to find words in his tiles so he tends to choose short words and spell them incorrectly at times. He often asks whether a word he sees exists and how to spell it. He asks if *zep* is a word, because there is an open *P* on the board and a double-word tile near it. I say no, but *zap* and *zip* are, if he has an *A* or an *I*. He does not, so he passes his turn and exchanges two of his letters in hopes of getting one of these vowels. When he still does not have them on the next turn he again passes and again exchanges a tile, preferring to wait for the perfect move than to take a lesser one along the way.

Vinny keeps score, placing each turn's score in a horizontal list on the paper and having a hard time adding them to find the winner. He loses track of the score at some time in each game. After five or six rounds he usually forgets to write my score in his attempt to find his next word; he writes his own score for another round or two, then forgets to write that as well. One game, I find a seven-letter word in my tiles on the first round; he decides we will play this time without keeping track of score.

At Pickup Sticks:
He quickly sees that there is one black stick among the many multicolored ones, and he announces that he wants that one. He ignores all the other sticks—in fact, he does not even notice sticks he has left alone far from all others in his dogged attempt to get the black stick from a crowded stack. When he gives up his turn he leaves me the lone stragglers but assures that I will not be able to get the black one. I win, but he ends up with the black stick.

At Sorry:
He plays by the rules most of the time. He allows me to "sorry" him, but his next move always involves a way to "sorry" me.

I am ahead, with two of my pieces close to Home and he with two pieces still at Start. He slides his way around the board so that he sends one of mine back to Start. He gets his piece out of Start by proper count, then leaves it there until he gets a "4 backwards" card—the only card that offers a short-cut to Home. While waiting, he gets all his other pieces around the board and into Home, then moves them out and back in again over and over until his "4 backwards" card appears.

These are further examples of Vinny's game playing, all showing some variation on his careful, nonrisky style of playing Life. In Scrabble he plays cautiously, double-checking before he uses any word he is not quite sure of. We see another aspect of his careful play here, in his preference for patiently waiting for the best move rather than try anything else; when he does not have the word he wants he passes and trades in letters until he does have it, losing whatever points he might have earned along the way. This aspect also shows up in pickup sticks, where he goes doggedly after the high-scoring black stick to the exclusion of all others, and in Sorry, where he waits for the "4 backwards" card rather than take his chances of moving around the board. When he keeps score in Scrabble he would rather play for nothing than chance losing after my particularly strong first move. In all these games Vinny keeps his eye on the perceived prize—a Life card for future benefit, a high-scoring word, a high-scoring stick, a short cut to the finish—and chooses to wait for that guaranteed success rather than take chances on other options. He is always calm about his playing, coolly waiting for his ship to come in.

Is his game playing indicative of his outside life? We would assume so, because it is so consistent across games and sessions, and we can interpret his game-playing dynamics simply because they are visible to us in the session. "You really like to wait for the best choice" and "You don't like to take chances" are accurate descriptions of Vinny, given the dynamics he has shown.

It happens, of course, that others in Vinny's life have the same view of him. His teachers say he is quiet and thoughtful, rarely volunteering until he is sure he has the right answer. His parents describe him as not wanting to try new experiences or change his mind once he takes a position. His most pressing presenting problem is his bottling up his feelings, appearing calm and cool until he explodes—not with anger, though, but with withdrawal. He stays in his room or in his shell until he feels better, just as he stays still in his games until he gets the good outcome he hopes for. In both cases he does not work on the outcome (he does not express his dissatisfaction in life; he does not manipulate the cards in Sorry or the tiles in Scrabble), he just stoically waits. This is observable, and therefore available to be worked with, in his game play in treatment even without knowledge of his outside life.

Let us look at some other examples of the way children might express themselves in structured games and the way in which therapists might learn to understand them through the board games.

## FOCUSED PLAY

Tessa plays many games but gravitates to Chutes and Ladders, both after playing other games in each session and as her exclusive game after trying others for several sessions.

> She takes out Chutes and Ladders and plays almost according to rule, spinning a second time or miscounting her moves when necessary to avoid chutes and reach ladders. We do not speak while we play. If I attempt to discuss her life or even the game, she tells me to hurry up and play. If I do not count fast enough she counts out my spaces for me.
>
> Weeks later, Tessa plays only Chutes and Ladders throughout each session. She continues to refuse to allow me to speak. She announces "Good!" when she falls down the giant chute in the center of the board, as this will allow her to climb up the giant ladder a few spaces away, ending nearly at her previous prechute position. At this point in our work she always starts her piece on square 1, where there is a ladder,

counting this as Start—so she always moves to square 38 before calling 39 "2," 40 "3," and so on. After playing this way for a few sessions, she begins to take all ladders on the game, so she completes the course with minimal moves, winning in a rout each time. When she wins each game, she—on the same spin that she reaches 100—starts at 1 (actually 38) again, until we lose track of how many laps we have taken.

Tessa's game play might seem dry and unproductive were it not for the characteristic way she goes about it. In her choice of Chutes and Ladders she demonstrates the reticence to display any emotional content: The game requires counting to the exclusion of all other interaction, and she plays it to the exclusion of all others. Her method of play, also, is one that insists on silence and attention only to counting—we are not to allow time or attention to any experience or emotion she might be having.

After a while she begins to play more creatively in the way she bends the box-top rules. She expresses pleasure even at her misfortune, because she imagines that it allows her good luck in the future. She begins on a ladder and eventually maneuvers her piece so that she takes all ladders, paralleling her style in outside life of looking for the silver lining of every potential cloud and insisting that no one around her suggest otherwise. Her presenting problem was that she was deeply distressed by her parents' sudden, painful separation; she showed this in temper tantrums, crying fits and nervous habits, while denying that she had any reaction. Tessa's board-game play demonstrated the same dynamics as her behavior at home: She insisted that everything was wonderful, even redefining drawbacks to be advantages. In the game, this technique worked for her better than in life! In any event, her creative play allows me to use her game-playing method as information about her dynamics and grist for the psychotherapeutic mill:

> *Tessa:* (landing on the long slide down from number 87 to number 24) Good!
> *JB:* Why is that good? It looks pretty bad to me.
> *T:* Because I have a chance to land here (pointing to number 28, where there is a ladder back to number 84).
> *JB:* Oh. So even a bad thing has a good side to it. It's hard to just think about bad things without any good side.
> *T:* Yes, now SPIN!

My comment is within her game and not directly about her outside life; for instance, I do not mention her unconvincing claim that she feels glad her father was getting a new apartment because it meant she had two homes instead of one. However, I also do not specifically not mention it; that is, I do not say that bad things *in the game* have good sides. I can think about her life, Tessa can think about the game or her life; both are true for her, and her understanding either one will help her in both.

## CREATIVELY RESTRUCTURED PLAY

Kal is a young 5-year-old not really ready for structured games but with a budding interest in the board games in the cabinet.

He takes out the Ungame and looks over the various pieces. After examining the board he chooses a playing piece and assigns me the color he wants me to use. He lines up all the other pieces behind our two. He hands a pile of assignment cards and one of the dice to me, and keeps a pile of cards and the other die in front of himself. He asks where to start the game, which direction he is supposed to move, and how to arrive at each of the special destinations. After he has asked about every aspect of the game he tosses his die to move. He announces as he gets to a crossroad that he will go one direction, I am to go another; the first one to arrive at his designated spot (closer to his direction than mine!) is the winner. As we play for a few moves, he tells me the rules have changed, and that I am to jump across the board to the square he prefers and stay there. The winning destination has changed also. When we have 5 minutes left in the session, he announces that he would like to stop playing and make a mess—following our usual ending routine.

Kal's play, like Tessa's, might seem at first glance to be unrevealing. He is clearly not able to play within the structure of the game, even as unstructured a game as the Ungame. The fact that he is interested at all is a sign of some conflict he is struggling with—perhaps his struggle over maturing into a child who could use board games, perhaps his interest in the rules that he finds imposed on him in his world, perhaps his wish to get me to take everything out of the closet to reach the one thing he wants.

His interest in rules is observable in the way he goes about this game: He sets up purposefully; I get one pile of cards, he gets one, I get one die, he gets one. He asks many questions about the box-top rules. Although he cannot fully follow them yet, he definitely wants to have all the rules clearly defined for him. While we play, he—like most children in treatment—becomes unable to stay within the assigned structure of the game. His method of dealing with this is to create new rules, equally structured and complex. After a time he redefines these rules as well, never eliminating the structure but rather always creating new structure. This would indicate that the rules are important to him even in his inability to follow them. His behavior at the end of the session demonstrates what happens when there is no way he can change the rules: He becomes vengeful—he destroys the order of the game and makes a mess that I have to clean up. And he is somewhat out of control—he becomes wild and frantic as he messes.

Kal's life patterns illustrate this same style of interest in structure and inability to follow externally imposed rules. His presenting problems included difficulties in leaving activities in his preschool program and at home. His parents had learned to let him dictate the family's schedule and described him creating long lists of rules for everyone to follow, changing them into different but equally complex lists along the way. These aspects of Kal's character style can be interpreted in his therapy because it is observable in his game playing as well as in his outside life:

*Kal:* I'm gonna go this way, and you have to go that way. If you get to this house, you win.

*JB:* You want me to have to go the way you say.

*K:* (takes his turn, lands on "if you cheered up someone, go to Cheerful Chalet") I didn't ever do that. . . . Where's Cheerful Chalet? . . . I did cheer up someone. When Jason in my class knocked over his block tower, I said that doesn't matter.

*JB:* You want to go over there [Cheerful Chalet], and you want to say whatever you have to to get there.

*K:* Now you have to go the other way, the way I went.

*JB:* I'm so confused. First, it seems like the rules are one way, then they're all changed and different. (I start to move.)

*K:* No, you have to go over here [Fearful Forest], and then go this way.

*JB:* And there are so many rules I can't keep them all straight. It's hard to know what I can do that would be the right thing. (He smiles.) Ooh, I think you *like* making me feel that way!

In this example, I have described Kal's use of rules in the game and attempted to portray what I think are his experiences of the rules imposed on him by his world. His rules are particularly noteworthy in the Ungame, which has no rules for which direction to go, whether to move to various locations (the instructions all ask "If you . . ." and one always has the option of claiming the experience or not), or who wins. Kal's world is full of rules, so he creates them for the Ungame. It is my understanding that he does follow rules in life when and only when he feels he has something immediate to gain from doing so, the way he describes having cheered someone up only after he decides he wants to go to the space offered. His description of the cheering is not very believable, particularly because he is noted for inconsiderate play in the block area at school, but the fact that he can identify this as appropriate behavior is a strength, even if he is not yet able to actually exhibit the behavior. I have not remarked on this in the example above, have not commented on the content of his answer at all. While I could have and in the treatment eventually expected to, at that moment in the game I felt that Kal was most absorbed in the aspect of his play pertaining to rules. I felt the most pressing issue in this particular play was the way he created the rules, more rules, and even more rules, and changed them arbitrarily as we played. I believe this is his experience of the rules in the world he lives in: He feels authorities create arbitrary rules, hundreds of them, that change frequently and without notice. My comments during the game, as if I were experiencing his rules as numerous and incomprehensible, are my attempt to describe Kal's sense of his world—the world he imposed on me during his play. My not being able to keep them all straight and not knowing what would be right parallel Kal's experience at school and at home; I wanted him to know that I understood that, that I felt that in the metaphor of the game. He, in turn, could feel a hostile pleasure in being the more powerful one, probably in the way he imagined authorities in his life felt pleasure in dominating over him. I remarked on this as well, within the game.

## ANXIOUS PLAY

Harvey is playing Mastermind. He has created the code; I am trying to guess it. I make a pattern of pegs and wait for him to consider it—a process that seems difficult for him to concentrate on long enough to find an answer. He finally tells me what he believes is the correct evaluation. I think about his response and compose a new guess, beginning with a red peg. "No," he says. "Don't use red." I reluctantly remove the red peg and try a white one. Harvey says, "These two (pointing to the red and white pegs in my previous guess) are wrong, and these two (blue and green) are right." I put a blue and a green peg out, but he corrects my placement.

We play Pictionary. I—a very poor artist—draw a circle with four stick legs attached. He says he does not know the answer—I should tell him. I ask him to wait, that he will be able to guess in a minute. He says he cannot. I add a two-legged stick figure astride the first figure and Harvey, with visible relief, shouts, "A horse!"

He draws a large rectangle with a line through it. I am stumped. I guess: "A building? A tall building? Something big and tall? Ummmm . . ." He says, "It's something that grows outside. It's big. It has leaves," giving me numerous verbal clues (illegal according to game directions) until I guess a tree.

Harvey, 10 years old, is old enough to follow box-top rules and to be able to wait for a moment or two. By temperament, however, he is not. He shows his anxiety in the way he quickly gives up in Pictionary, announcing before I have completed even a rudimentary drawing that he will fail. I am willing to struggle with my picture until he can comprehend it, but he is not. When he gives clues in both these games, he cannot seem to bear the silence while I consider my play. He rapidly gives me far more verbal clues than are permitted by the rules or than I have asked for. It is impulsive behavior but not acting-out aggression—more an anxious spilling of his ideas.

This anxious worry about failure seen in his board-game play is indeed what has brought Harvey into treatment. We can work with it in the game by discussing his worries as they arise in Mastermind and Pictionary because they are representative of the worries he experiences in school and at home. When we have conquered his worries on the game board we will be well on our way to helping him with them in outside life as well.

## AGGRESSIVE PLAY

A short, slim, limber 9-year-old, Peter plays the card game of Spit. He sets up the cards expertly, an old hand at the game, and calls the first "One, two, three, Spit!" We both play an animated round. The second call is faster than the first, slurring the numbers together as he shouts, and the third is an instant "Spit!" without prelude. While he sits patiently on one hand for the first round and insists that I sit on mine as well to enforce the one-hand-only rule of the game, he soon has both hands and his whole body involved in the play. He adds a card to his pile and starts spitting on it before I have finished looking at or spitting on the round before. If he and I each have a card to play on the same pile, he either gets there first or removes my card to replace it with his own. When he can play no more (he has finished his deck long before I have finished mine), he grabs the smaller of the two piles—again before I have finished playing my cards onto it—and starts the next round. Throughout, he is jumping up and down and using his whole body to play.

Peter plays Checkers with less athletic involvement. He sets up the board and goes first. After my first jump of his piece he jumps two of mine—skipping an empty space in the process. When I am close to transforming a piece to a king, he comes from behind to remove that piece from the board. He jumps forward and backward, over one or two of my pieces at a time, quickly demanding king status for all his pieces and eliminating all of mine.

Peter plays his games aggressively. In Spit, he is bodily as well as emotionally absorbed in the game, consistently pushing his moves in front of mine by speed or by force. He does not argue or complain, he just physically enforces his wishes. In Checkers, too, he is a bully about the way he plays. He moves wherever he likes, conquering my checkers with the force of his might. He is not physically mighty here—he does have the ego strength to remain within the metaphor of the checkerboard—but he clearly overpowers me.

In Peter's case, as in the others presented throughout this book, it is possible to work with him on issues that arise in his game without probing his outside life at all. As it usually happens, his outside life parallels his gameplay: He is a bully there as well. He is the tiny son of a large, weightlifting father who enforces harsh discipline by severe physical punishment. Peter then goes to school and tries to be equally stern with his classmates and is far too physical on the playground. His board-game play shows the same wish to overcome his powerlessness with his father by becoming all powerful with others.

*Peter:* (quadruple jumping—illegally—my checkers) Hah! I got you!

*JB:* Wow! You *really* got me; *four* of me.

*P:* Hah!

*JB:* You love it when you get me that way.

*P:* You bet!

*JB:* You really need to get me that way, way more than I ever could get you.

*P:* Right!

*JB:* It's important for you to be the strongest one, to really destroy me.

*P:* Right! Like my father does!

91

*JB:* When you're strong here, against me, you can feel as powerful as you think your father does against you—and you can make me feel as weak as you feel when you're with him.
*P:* Right!

In my work with Peter, I describe his power in the games he plays, remarking on the way he can make me feel like there is no hope for me because he is so strong and good at what he does. Peter is pleased to hear this, and he is eventually able to verbalize the fact that he feels this way with his father. Peter's treatment does end in discussing his life outside the therapy room once we begin the process of understanding and interpreting his experiences solely through the structured games he plays. I have followed Peter's lead: He showed me his dynamics in the board game rather than by describing his life with his father, so I discussed his play in the board game. Only when he took the lead in describing his experiences outside the playroom did I accompany him in this exploration.

## DEFENSIVE PLAY

Nadine plays behind my back, or, to be more accurate, I play behind hers. She sets up all her play, board games as well as dramatic play, with her back to me and her body between me and her play. When she plays dramatically, she often makes voices for the characters under her breath so that I cannot hear.

We play Go Fish with cards one day. Her small hands cannot quite hold all the cards she has, so she puts them on the floor—again, behind her back—and surreptitiously picks up a corner of each card to see what she has. I ask for 8s, but she has none. Two turns later, she asks me for 8s. I assume she has picked one in the interim . . . until the game continues and three more 8s appear in my hand.

Len plays a variety of games. As a reading-disabled 10-year-old, he prefers games with minimal reading and often mixes words or simply replaces them with his own inventions. He still enjoys Candyland, because no reading is involved, so he could not be embarrassed by his difficulty. When he plays, though, he takes out the cards for special destinations—the Lollypop Forest, the Gumdrop Swamp, and so on—except the Snowflake Princess card, which he keeps for his first turn.

He plays Sorry at times, but cannot read the backward or split moves. He removes "Sorry" cards, or places them at the bottom of the deck when he comes to them.

Both of these children are playing defensive games. Nadine plays so that I cannot see or hear her, both in her character stories and in keeping Go Fish cards behind her back. She has secrets in the way she asks for 8s without having any of her own. This is a style that probably developed in response to her need to get away from her ever present mother, and that is now a part of her character style, visible in her play and her structured game play. I describe this to her, saying that she hides everything so nobody else can see what only she will know about, that she has secrets that only she can know. I am thinking about both her game and her life, speaking in general terms that neither restrict themselves to the game nor specifically include references outside the game. One could be more explicit in describing Nadine's life; it is not my preference to do so with her, because she has not responded as well to my direct comments as to my generic remarks about the dynamics she shows me. In any event, the description of her defensive, secretive style applies to both her game and her life; she plays it, I generically describe it, and she internalizes my interpretation for both. Eventually, she becomes able to try out showing me more of herself—again in both her game and her life—in preparation for showing other people in her life as well.

Len defends against confronting any setbacks. In avoiding an encounter with his learning disability, he chooses games that require little or no reading. He removes cards from the Candyland and Sorry decks to prevent his having to go backward once he has begun on his way. His fear of losing ground can be interpreted solely through his game play, as it appears in the treatment. It is clear from the games he plays and the ways he plays them that he is afraid of failure, uncomfortable with his insufficiencies, and too timid to take risks in his life. I describe this to him as I see it in his play. I remark as he takes out a game that he has chosen a game that is made for young children (Candyland) or that will be easy for him to read (Sorry). As he removes unwanted cards I note that he is doing so, saying I see that he will guarantee that he never has to go backward, that he will be sure he will never have to start all over, that he is taking the scary, risky part away. Len can hear my comments as descriptive of his playing style and his approach to life in general. As he hears me, he understands himself better and trusts me with more of these aspects of himself. Gradually, Len, like most children I play with, begins to try out some frightening changes in the game: He leaves one or two special cards in the deck just to see what will happen. (Because he understands that "cheating" is acceptable with me—see Chapter 4—he is free to refuse the card if he picks it when he is not ready.) He even tries games with reading involved, letting me read to him or trying out his own shaky reading skill. Once I have interpreted his defensive style in his game play, Len understands himself and can begin to change, both in his play and in his life.

## FEARFUL PLAY

Belinda, 10 years old, chooses a variety of games. She still plays Candyland, remarking that she used to play this "when I was little" each time she takes it out. She plays Sorry, but she decides not to "Sorry" me, claiming afterward that she did not see the opportunity. We play Connect Four; she places her pieces next to mine, blocking my connections but not looking for her own. When she chooses Spit, she waits for me to move first before she plays any cards. After we have both taken our first round we look for any moves we might have missed. We both have a Jack to play on the pile showing a 10; she waits for me to see mine and reach for it before she reaches for hers.

Belinda is a fearful child playing a fearful game style. She enjoys the regressive experience of becoming a little girl playing Candyland. She plays all of her games carefully, watching me and defending against my winning but not making offensive moves herself. She shows the same wary style in her game play as she does in life, where she has been described as afraid of her own shadow. She is worried about possible retaliation from me and loss of my love just as she worries—somewhat more appropriately—about the retaliation from an angry foster mother and the loss of several foster mothers before her. Belinda and I could talk about her worries as a frequently abandoned foster child, or we can discuss the clear expression on the game board of her worries that she will not be liked.

Until she is developmentally ready to engage in verbal treatment, Belinda responds better to discussion of her game playing. I tell her that I notice how carefully she watches me as she plays, that she plays just well enough to beat me but not by too much, that she waits for me to make a move before she makes one herself. Again, the description of Belinda's game play is that same description one would make of her lifestyle; as she hears me describe it, she can consider herself and her options—on the game board and off.

Carl, described in Chapter 4 as he played Candyland to lose—or almost lose—is another example of this kind of fearful play. Carl seems by his playing style to be worried about what will happen to him if he plays too aggressively. He pulls his punches in order to give his playmate a fighting chance, although his self-esteem will not allow him to lose altogether. Belinda, older than Carl, seems to be a better game player, and she sometimes chooses games with a greater skill component. But their styles of playing with very little offense are similar.

## CONCLUSION

In this chapter I have tried to show that structured board games are full of psychodynamic meaning. Children's choices in the games they prefer and the styles with which they play reveal information about their psychological states, the difficulties they face in their outside life, and the family systems from which they come. If we play vigilantly, allowing children to demonstrate their own characteristic styles rather than imposing our own and observing the dynamics that children display rather than trying to play our own best game, we can use the structured board games therapeutically and to the advantage of the latency-age children we are seeing in the playroom.

# CHAPTER SIX

# Development of Game Play

Five-year-old Kevin plays pickup sticks:

He throws the sticks—sometimes straight up in the air, sometimes around the room, sometimes down from a standing position—and we are to rush around picking up as many as we can as quickly as we can. Kevin shoves me out of his way with his elbows, his shoulders, his whole body to grab sticks, giggling gleefully as he does. He leaves two or three within my reach, but races me and pushes me so that he can get almost all for himself. I pretend to race for the sticks, but I stand or crawl to get them, leaving me at a disadvantage compared to his small, quick, more flexible stature. I dramatically "lose" each stick to him and talk about how impossible he is to beat. As he first takes out the game I announce that he will win and I will get only a few sticks because he is always sure to make it happen that way. He laughs as I describe his play and his guarantee of winning.

Seven-year-old Mary plays pickup sticks:

> She takes the box of sticks to the floor and sits with them, then drops them out of the box onto the floor. They fall in a fairly close pattern. Mary goes first. She picks up two and three sticks at a time—if they are touching or leaning against each other, she picks up the whole pile. She carries the sticks she has already picked up in her hand, knocking them around so they hit and move the sticks still on the floor. Her hands, feet, and knees move sticks as she wriggles around trying to get in position to pick up the next pile. I rarely get a turn, except the two or three outlying sticks she occasionally leaves for me. I describe her method of getting "so many" sticks herself and leaving so few for me; she agrees with me. She says she is very good at this, but her brother is better. She also says "He never lets me win him," and he sometimes hits her with the sticks.

Nine-year-old Arty plays pickup sticks:

> He wonders why the floor is the best place to play, then tests the table (they fall off) and the rug (they get caught in the pile, or the pressure on the rug moves them) before sitting on the floor to cast the sticks. He does not like the first two throws, so he continues until he achieves the right balance of pile to stray sticks. Arty goes first. He picks up sticks one at a time, carefully. He does move other sticks, minimally, but ignores that until he has a handful of sticks. He then asks me if he

100

moved. I respond honestly, and I get a turn. I pick up the stray stick he had missed, then try for one on a pile but notice the bottom stick moving, so I stop and give Arty a turn.

Thirteen-year-old Davida plays pickup sticks:

She asks if I want to play, then takes out the sticks and sits on the floor with them. We choose sticks to see who goes first. I win the draw, so she throws the sticks and I begin. I pick up three stray sticks, then move on my first attempt at the pile. She also moves on her attempt, and we alternate short turns. During my turn, she says she has been swamped with home-work lately, and her mother is "on my case again" about religion. Davida's mother is deeply religious; Davida thinks herself an atheist; they argue passionately and often, to save the other from what they believe to be a dangerous position. Davida enjoys egging her mother on to fury, but says this time she stopped herself because she noticed how much she hurt her mother. She describes the interaction in which her mother asked her to pray, Davida tried to think of prayer-like words she could utter without feeling hypocritical or ashamed. She says she is starting to give up on ever convincing her mother of the acceptability of her position—a realization that leaves her deeply saddened over her unrequited wish for a close relation-ship with a loving mother. We sit on the floor, each holding a handful of pickup sticks, neither moving toward the game, while we talk about Davida's experiences and feelings. At the end of the session, we put the sticks back—without counting score—and she leaves the room.

These are four examples of age-appropriate game play, illustrating the normal expected development of the use of structured games.

## PRELATENCY BOARD-GAME PLAY

Kevin, at 5, is prelatency and just starting to be interested in the structured play of board games. He chooses board games—here, pickup sticks—from the toy cabinet. He sets up a game where we compete against each other. There are rules and requirements; there will be a specific and clear-cut end of the play, and one of us will win and one will lose. This is in contrast to his earlier play, and that typical of younger children, in which Kevin chose dollhouse or action figures and created dramatic scenes of jumping, yelling, feeding, bathing, shooting, and throwing characters off roofs and out windows. Indeed, he continues to alternate his game play with dramatic play, often treating the game board as his dollhouse or battlefield.

Even when he does choose a structured game he is only beginning to be able to play it. He wants rules, but he is not yet able to follow them for long. He wants to compete with me, but he is not yet able to bear the possibility that I might win. He wants structure, but he cannot yet play without running or jumping around the room. So we play at Kevin's age level: We use structured game materials at times; we set up the board or throw the sticks; we play at playing the game. But he beats me by muscling me out or demanding that he have all the advantages.

My play matches Kevin's developmental level. I agree to a structured game and dramatically pretend to get ready to play. I announce that he will win—that he always wins—or that this time I intend to get more sticks than he. I run—not my fastest—and grab—not my hardest—while pretending to be gathering lots and lots of sticks. I elaborately count out the paltry few sticks I am holding at the end of each round, and describe his particular style of getting more and more excited as he plays and how difficult it is for him to hold still or stay quiet when that happens to him. Neither of us is playing a structured game here; we are dramatically and physically acting out what at other times has been played out in action figures. Kevin has been able to symbolize the struggle using wood sticks gathered rather than toy guns shot, but is not developmentally able to make the further step of struggling within the metaphor of the proper game structure itself.

## EARLY-LATENCY BOARD-GAME PLAY

Seven-year-old Mary is somewhat further along the developmental spectrum, as befits her somewhat older age. She chooses from the toy closet and sets up a close approximation of the structure of the box-top game.

Interestingly, though, while Kevin is interested in all the board games and attempts to play each of them in turn, Mary picks only games she is capable of playing. So, while neither can read well yet, Kevin chooses reading games and asks to be read to or makes his own rules without reading, Mary only opts for games that do not require reading above her ability. This is partly characterological—Kevin often strives for more mature behavior while Mary is comfortable with a childish presentation—and partly developmental.

Mary is at a stage where she is attempting to understand game rules and play accordingly—so if she could not read assignment cards she could not play—while Kevin still makes up his own structure, so whether he can understand the official game cards is irrelevant.

Mary still needs physical activity in her play, so her favorite games are those that require full body movement, like pickup sticks. She uses the structure of the game in her wish for proper turn taking. She is not yet physically able to play, so she fails to pick up most sticks without moving others, and she is not yet psychologically able to allow luck and skill to take their course. So she insists on going first, and she ignores the signs that her turn should be over. She, like most children in therapy, needs to win. She accomplishes this by structuring the game entirely in her favor. She, like Kevin, alternates her choice of structured games with play with dramatic play materials. She picks clay at times or puppets or action figures, and creates scenes in which she reveals herself in expressive play.

My play is often limited to comments about her play. While Mary is at a stage of game play where structure is beginning to be relevant to her, she is still unable to fully comprehend the rules and the turn-taking aspects. Her alternating use of dramatic play materials informs me of this, as well as the way in which her play often evolves from a beginning structure—setting up the game, announcing the rules, deciding who will go first—into more dramatic play where the game characters dance or march or fight, or the clay is used for creating dinner for the puppets rather than for the structured game we started to play. I follow her play through its various structures. I comment on the way she is able to pick up many sticks each time, and on the fact that she is getting better at picking them up from complex piles without moving (when this is true). I make voices for the sticks or game pieces when she begins to play dramatically. In short, I follow her from structured game play to dramatic play and back, commenting on the game as she is playing it at each moment.

## MIDDLE-LATENCY BOARD-GAME PLAY

Arty illustrates the next stage of game-play development. He fully demonstrates the interest in the structured play that appropriately accompanies latency. He chooses structured games and only structured games, pausing only briefly to pick up guns or dinosaurs, then replace them and take out a game box in each session. He uses a variety of games, at times those that require skill or advanced abilities, at other times simpler games like Candyland or Chutes and Ladders—but he always chooses a board game. When we complete one within a session, he starts a second or third.

He uses the games the way the box-top suggests. He hands out money and playing pieces according to the rules, even throws dice to see who goes first most of the time.

He also needs to win. He accomplishes this, too, within the official rules of the game. Kevin wins by bodily pushing me away from the game or changing the rules to "my rules" of play. Mary wins by ignoring the rules that are inconvenient to her. Arty wins by rethrowing the sticks until the play can proceed according to the rules but in his favor—by asking to go first, by giving me a turn on time but holding me strictly to the rules and watching me closely for my mistakes. Even in altering the play so he can always be the winner, he never disregards the box-top rules. At his stage of development, he has fully incorporated rule play into his psyche and is unable to play as if the official rules did not exist, as 5-year-olds or 7-year-olds might.

My play with Arty is also according to the rules. I become involved in the game we are playing, "hoping" for the right card to come up or holding my breath as I dramatically try to get a stick from the pick-up-stick pile. I watch my own play carefully and give up my turn at the slightest quiver of the wrong stick, screaming playfully at myself for failing. I watch Arty's play as well, but I do not comment on his failures until he asks. When he does ask, I answer truthfully: "Yes, you moved the red stick"; "No, you didn't move the red stick but you did move the blue one"; or "I didn't see it move." This last comment is a useful, honest answer when I don't want to call him on a minor failure in an impossible stick layout or when I have been thinking about his dynamics or how to phrase my next interpretation and have truly not noticed whether he moved or not. Arty's need to win leads him to ask me whether he moved only every second or third miss (he never *says* he moved, only asks me, and only when he did indeed move!). I comment on his need to win and his playing in such a way as to be sure he will, as well as his difficulty admitting directly that he has failed. I discuss his skill, his increasing ability to pick up sticks carefully, his inventive tricks for getting difficult sticks, and his particular style of insisting on having one particular stick no matter where it lies in the pile. Occasionally, when I have something I need to bring up with him—a meeting with his parents, an upcoming vacation, some information I have received from his school—I mention this while we play. This is by way of communicating with him as well as gently raising the idea that he will soon be developing into a more verbal adolescent.

## EARLY-ADOLESCENT BOARD-GAME PLAY

Thirteen-year-old Davida has passed through latency and is well on her way to adolescence. The structured games are still important to her because she experiences herself as too old to play with toys and she is not yet able to face a full session of sitting in a chair and talking. So she takes out a game each week, a different game from a subset of games that require some level of knowledge or skill; she never chooses Candyland or Blockhead, for example.

She then applies herself to the game only partially, but fully within the box-top rules. It is not even a struggle for her to toss to see who goes first, or to give up her turn when she misses. While she sometimes seems involved in the competition and is proud of particularly good moves she makes, who wins—or even whether we complete the game within our time—seems largely irrelevant to her. The game is an excuse to sit on the floor and an available respite from talk that might become painful. She can always stop talking and pick up additional sticks if we get too close to something uncomfortable in our talk. But the treatment is becoming more and more about the talk. Davida is nearing emotional adolescence, when she will express herself and work out her difficulties verbally rather than behaviorally. At that point, she will be seen in adult-like talk therapy.

The board game for Davida is a transitional space, both developmentally and within each moment. She is developing transitionally from an age where she plays structured games for the sake of the structure and the game, expressing herself in the way she plays and working out her difficulties within the game itself, into an age where she is a more verbal adult. She is also, within each therapy session, attempting the difficult task of talking out what is on her

107

mind. She uses the game to make the transition from outside life into the therapy session, from separation into relating to me, from talking into quiet thinking (and taking her turn while she thinks).

My play with Davida matches hers. I choose sticks or toss dice, making comments about my winning or losing the toss. I take my turn—fairly—when it is time, wait patiently when it is hers. With Davida I rarely comment on the game itself because it is not the medium of treatment for her, as it is for Arty. When something unusual happens—a great word in Scrabble, a triple double (Go to Jail) in Monopoly, an unexpected concentration on the game rather than on our talk—I do comment on that. Otherwise, I talk with Davida about her experiences, empathizing or problem solving as appropriate to what she brings up. When she does stop talking to bury herself in the game, I often mention that she has done so, proposing the idea that the discussion may have become too anxiety provoking for her to continue. We then play the game for a turn or two or ten, until she seems ready to return to talking.

This progression, from Kevin to Mary to Arty to Davida—from five to seven to nine to thirteen—illustrates the development of structured game play: from dramatic play within the game, to dramatic play alternating with structured play, to structured play as the primary expression of issues, to the beginning of the ability and interest in verbal expression.

## SECOND SET OF EXAMPLES

Let us follow a second set of children, as an additional illustration of this common developmental process.

Five-year-old Kal plays Monopoly:

He asks what "this red box" is, asking for help taking it down from the bottom of a pile on a high shelf. He examines the board, asking me to read parts of it to him, then looks at game pieces, houses and hotels, Chance and Community Chest cards, property cards, and all denominations of money. He asks me to deal out money, "one of everything to each of us, no five of everything, because I'm five years old." He picks a playing piece and assigns me one. We each get one of the dice. He would like to deal out Chance cards as well, but finds the allotted space on the board and decides to put them there, reversing the two piles of Chance and Community Chest. He goes first, throws, elaborately finds the card that matches the property he has landed on. He wants a house on the property—a big red house, not a little green one. He picks up the dice and throws again, decides he wants to stop at the Railroad rather than continue counting, and tells me to take my turn. But before I finish counting he has thrown his die again and is moving on around the board. He is upset when he lands on Jail, even Just Visiting Jail, and wants to take another turn quickly to get past. We play until near the end of the session, when I give him my standard "five more minutes" warning. He gets a glint in his eye and tosses the board—game pieces, Chance cards, hotels and all—up in the air. He picks up the rest of the cards and money and tosses them across the room as well. He announces, "This game makes a good mess," and steps out of the room so that I can clean up what he has proudly created.

Eight-year-old Tessa plays Monopoly:

> She cannot decide what to play, so she takes out Monopoly,
> Sorry, and Chutes and Ladders, places them all on the table,
> and says, "Eenie, meenie, miney, moe" to choose. We set up the
> Monopoly board; she asks me which piece I would like to be
> before choosing her own, and we toss one die each to see who
> goes first. She gets a low number, so she tosses again until she
> gets a 6, then asks me to toss. She remembers clearly how much
> money we should each get and tells me how many bills to hand
> each of us. She takes one extra $500 bill for herself. She goes
> first, lands on Vermont Avenue, and decides not to buy it. I
> land just behind her on Oriental Avenue, and do buy it. She
> takes several turns before she buys a piece of property—
> landing on Community Chest and Free Parking before coming
> to something she finds strategically useful. I land on St.
> Charles Place and, before I can say anything, Tessa announces
> that I do not want it. Nor do I want Tennessee, she tells me, or
> any other property. We continue around the board, with Tessa
> carefully buying only the better pieces of land—announcing
> often how she really only wants Boardwalk—and me not
> permitted to purchase anything. She soon owns two sides of
> the board, charging me gleefully as I make my way through her
> territory with no income of my own. At the 5-minute warning,
> she quickly puts the game away, stuffing everything haphaz-
> ardly into the box, and takes out Chutes and Ladders. "I'll go
> first," she says as she pulls out the board and her favorite
> playing piece. Before I have chosen my piece, she has spun
> the wheel and counted out her first move. She tells me to
> hurry. We play out our last few minutes in almost silence,

spinning and counting, spinning and counting, spinning and counting . . .

Twelve-year-old Steve plays Monopoly:

He looks quickly at the array of games on the shelf, grabs the top game. We set up the board together, each putting cards on the board, choosing our own playing pieces, taking our own money. He places the bank on his side of the table. We toss to see who goes first. I win and toss the two dice for my move. Before I can move, he mentions his argument with his teacher the day before, resulting in his being called for detention and then being further punished by his strict father when he got home. We discuss his feelings about this for a few minutes—his innocence of the accusation his teacher leveled at him, his frustration in a class where he seems never to succeed, his wish that he could just once get his father to pay some positive attention to him. Steve asks whose turn it is, lets me count and buy Connecticut Avenue, then tosses the dice and starts his own move. He then continues with his story of the previous day: His "stupid mother" took his father's side, his "dumb brother" came home with an A on a spelling test, his only friend was the family dog—a mutt who frequently gets kicked or beaten when the father is angry. We continue through the session this way, talking until Steve asks us to play, playing until he begins to talk. When we have 5 minutes left, Steve looks at his own watch and starts to put the game away. We both put pieces back where they belong, sorting everything carefully and talking about Steve's difficulties as we do, until he leaves the room when he decides our time is up.

In this progression again, we have seen the typical development from prelatency dramatic play using a board game, into typical latency-age play exclusively within the structure of the game, and into adolescent talk therapy taking place over the top of a board game.

Kal uses the board game as he would a dollhouse. We set up the board, but he takes the property he wants and builds the kind of house he prefers on it. He wants the game taken down from the shelf—as opposed to setting this up with plastic houses and wooden cars—but he is not interested in the officially imposed structure of the game.

I play with Kal as if he were playing with houses and cars on the floor—exploring the territory, driving from place to place, "talking" to the person I visit in Jail. I comment on his interest in *big* houses and his fear of being even near the Jail.

Tessa is fully able to play the structured game as long as she wins. Like Arty, her game alterations accept the structure of the game even while she maneuvers to win. I am expected to move around the board when it is my turn; I am just forbidden to choose to buy any property. She throws the dice repeatedly or counts inaccurately to be sure she lands on the coveted Boardwalk—but she still throws the dice and counts her squares.

I play the game with Tessa. I marvel at her "luck" at landing on Boardwalk—"just like she wanted; as if she could make it happen by wishing." I express my frustration at not owning anything, remarking that I could have made money "if only I had bought Marvin Gardens" when I landed on it first. I suggest that I don't play the game very well if I don't own any property and can't make any money, and that she really understands the game better than I.

Steve, like Davida, shows an early adolescent use of the game.

112

He sets up the game according to the official rule book, then talks about his life as if the game were not there. When his life issues become too difficult to discuss he retreats to the safety of the game—selling me my property, moving his own piece, throwing the dice again—until his anxiety level falls enough to begin talking again.

I follow Steve's process, playing the game when he needs to but not pressing the game when he does not. I never tell him to move, but I quickly do when he asks me to. I discuss his issues when he talks, describe his increased anxiety when he retreats to the game, and enjoy the game moves as they occur. I try to make myself a comfortable companion so that he is free to attempt the talk therapy he struggles for, then interpret the material he shares with me verbally.

In addition to developmental level, these children's personal issues can be seen in the ways they play their games and spend their time.

Kal is a child who needs to have his own way at all things, at home and at school as well as in treatment. His insisting on playing a game above his skill level, on having the bottom game from the pile, on landing on the square he likes best and choosing the kind of house he wants (and not paying for it!) all demonstrate his style of taking what he wants and expecting that his wishes will be granted. I comment on this as he plays. His behavior at the end of the session, when he cannot bear to hear the 5-minute warning without throwing the game, illustrates the kind of behavior his teachers describe as becoming uncontrollable at transition times in school. His expecting me to clean up his mess shows his belief that he will be waited on—well founded, based on his experiences at home—and his inability to be present while I clean shows that he has some conflict

113

over his wishes. I discuss these observations as I watch him make his mess and begin to clean it up.

Tessa also needs her own way. She uses the board-game structure in the way she takes all the property for herself and forbids me to own any but the least desirable. When the 5-minute warning occurs she can no longer have her own way—which would be to continue to play until I was bankrupt. She quickly—because it is too painful—throws the game away, but in a more controlled way than Kal who needs to throw the game everywhere. Then, in her characterological style, she buries herself in the structure of a game with no emotional content. She counts, I count, she counts, I count, in a kind of rhythmic drone that calms her in the 5 minutes before she leaves the room. This allows her to meet her mother in the waiting room with a cheerful "Hi! That was fun!" as if she had not been disappointed, in my office or in her life. I discuss Tessa's difficulty approaching the end of the session and her comfort in the easy play of Chutes and Ladders, as well as her need to leave the session and approach her life in a continual good mood.

Steve does not need to win the game. As with Davida, the game is irrelevant to the content of his treatment. His particular issues can be seen in the life he describes, and this can be discussed verbally. It can also be seen in the times he retreats to the game, which he does more frequently than Davida. I mention the importance of these moments and the connection to what he had been talking about before that. Steve is a person who tries to control himself and his life. At the end of his session, he is the one to give the 5-minute warning and start cleaning up so that I do not impose this on him. At the end of the session he declares time up—always just a moment before I would have to—and leaves the room himself, again to take for himself the little bit of control over his surroundings that he has available to him. I describe this process to him as well.

In this chapter, we have seen the way in which children normally grow from the dramatic, physical play of young childhood into the structured play of latency and later into the verbal expressiveness of adolescence and adulthood. In my own play I attempt to match each child's needs in the style of their play and the psychological needs of their treatment, and also in the developmental level of use of structured games.

## GENDER DIFFERENCES

A word seems in order here about gender differences in game play. There are both males and females represented in this chapter as well as throughout the book. It has been my experience that, while both sexes do use board games and progress through similar stages of game play, boys tend to be game players more frequently during sessions and for longer in their development.

There are at least two reasons for this. First, boys in this society are still socialized to be more competitive than girls. They are expected to be more aggressive sports players—and children are signed up for soccer and baseball leagues at younger and younger ages these days. While the gender difference may change as a new generation of children grows up playing in girls' leagues from age 3 and watching women in positions of sports accomplishment or political leadership, it still seems the case that boys are encouraged and permitted to be more competitive on the whole. The advice to "be nice" and "just have fun, don't worry about winning or losing" seems to be offered to young girls more than boys.

Second, girls tend to be more accomplished verbally at younger ages. So they may pass more quickly through the stage of structured game play. They play with dolls and action figures and dinosaurs at young ages just as boys do, and then move into more interest in rule-oriented game play. But as they become more skilled at verbal expression they move out of this stage and into the stage of talking out their difficulties at younger ages. Again, this may change as society learns to encourage girls to be more physically active and allows them to be more assertive, and to encourage boys to be more emotionally expressive and allows them to be more sensitive.

# CHAPTER SEVEN

# *But Is It Therapy?*

Adena, 10 years old, plays board games for most of every session. Today we are playing Monopoly. She is a very careful player, buying most but not all of the property she lands on. She prefers the certainty of utilities and railroads to the major investments of monopolies with houses and hotels. She works one set of properties at a time, hoping (or arranging!) to land on all railroads or all properties of a given color on consecutive turns. She tries to own enough valuable property so that I pay her more money when I land on her holdings than she pays when she lands on mine.

We can make several observations from this example of structured game play in this young girl. First, by the fact that she plays board games so frequently—and she plays them fully, using the box-top rules to set up the game and even cheating within the rules, by moving the dice to land on the wished-for space—we understand that she is developmentally in the structured-game-playing latency stage. We note that she is highly focused, in the way she concentrates on one accomplishment at a time. We can see that she prefers safe bets (railroads and utilities) to riskier or longer-term investments. We notice that she is aware of how she stands relative to me and that she is competitive in her play.

So we can use Adena's game-playing strategies to give us information about her developmental progress and her psychological make-up. But how can we use it for therapy? Even if we were to describe to her what we know about her based on her play, how would that help her? We could make comments such as the following:

You know a lot about the rules and ways to play this game.

You're working hard to get just the properties you want, and you don't care about any of the other ones.

You really want to have more, better stuff than me.

How would these comments be useful to Adena? How can we turn this understanding of children's dynamics into a system of treatment that is therapeutic? This chapter will show the therapy offered to Adena and the way it seemed to help her, through following her Monopoly play over the course of several months of treatment. She plays other games as well and has some beginning abilities to verbalize some of the issues that concern her, but her Monopoly playing will be concentrated on here in an attempt to show the therapeutic process through one child's course of play with a single game.

## BEGINNING GAME PLAY

Adena is a quiet girl whom parents and teachers describe as cooperative and eager to please. She has many friends and many classmates who want her to be their friend. She fights occasionally with
her older sister but is more likely to be the victim than the aggressor.
She was brought into treatment because her parents feared for her
overeagerness and her self-esteem. They described her as upset over
playing second to her sister's accomplishments and over her inability to turn down a play date or refuse a classmate anything. One
classmate, in particular, seems to want to be Adena's friend more
than Adena wants to be hers, and has "borrowed" many of Adenas
clothes, including a favorite woolen hat, without returning them.
Adena is uncomfortable with this arrangement but is unable to
extricate herself or her belongings.

In Adena's Monopoly play we see evidence of these presenting
problems. Her clear competitiveness with me is transferred from her
feelings about her sister. Her difficulty hurting me, as she fears to
hurt her friends, can be seen in this example, repeated here from
Chapter 4:

> . . . I have very little cash. I land on Tennessee Avenue, with
> a hotel, requiring me to pay her $950. She insists that I pay her
> only $900 because that is all the cash I have. On my next turn
> I have received some income from her paying me on her turn,
> but it is not enough for the $1,100 I owe her for Illinois
> Avenue rent. She wants me to skip the turn, not to pay her, to
> pay her from the bank rather than from my own assets.

She seems as worried about taking all my money as she is about
refusing her classmates' requests. She wants desperately to be liked,

by her peers, her parents, and her therapist, and she is afraid that if she sticks up for her own wishes we will not like her. This, then—her worry over asserting herself lest she be disliked—is an important focus of Adena's therapy, conducted in her game playing.

In these first games, I remark simply about her style, describing her game play as described above and mentioning her worry about crossing me. When she repeatedly refuses the rent I owe her, I repeatedly comment on this. I say, "You don't want me to run out of money." "You're worried about what will happen to you if I go bankrupt." "You want to win this game, but you are worried about winning by too much." "You're afraid about how I might react if you take all my money and all my property."

At that point in Adena's treatment it was not my preference to relate these interpretations to her outside life. I noted to myself that her worries with me matched her worries with her classmates—that she worried about taking my money in the same way that she worried over saying no to a play date asked of her; that she went on the play date and let me keep my Monopoly money even though both were opposite to her own wishes; that she regretted the play dates while still trying to make them fun for her classmates, and probably also regretted her style of Monopoly play with me. Another therapist might just as well say these things directly to Adena; I was not inclined to work outside the metaphor of the game she was playing, especially in the early weeks of treatment. My preference was to describe her play and the concerns I saw expressed there.

This seemed to be enough for her, for over the next few weeks and months Adena's game playing changed gradually. She continued for some time to play carefully and considerately, making decisions and cheating so as to stay just ahead of me but never allowing herself to trounce me; I continued to describe this mode of play to her.

Then she experimented with a new idea.

## FIRST VARIATION

A few weeks later, as we are slowly working to build up our holdings, Adena changes the rules in mid-game. She decides spontaneously to play "backward": We will deal out all properties and give them back when we land on them! The winner will be the one with the least money or property when we stop.

This is an interesting variation on the game; for Adena it represents a significant psychological breakthrough. The spontaneity of her decision is an accomplishment for a child who is usually so carefully thoughtful about every choice. Her willingness to reverse the rules represents a new ability to refuse to do what she is supposed to do. And the idea to give back property is her attempt to see what it feels like to take and give away, and what it might be like to ask her classmate to return her clothes. She can see what she feels like in asking me to put my holdings back, how I react to her demands, and can vicariously understand how her classmate might feel in giving back her clothes. I try to describe these experiments:

*Adena:* It'd be really funny to play backward! What if we had to lose a property when we landed there. . . . Then we'd like it if we *didn't* have any property!
*JB:* That *would* be funny. That would be a whole different way to play.

121

*A:* You want to try it?

*JB:* It's up to you.

*(This is something of a shared joke, because Adena asks me frequently what I want to do, and I always say; "It's up to you.")*

*A:* Let's try it!

*JB:* That's a whole new idea—you're going to change everything right in the middle. Wow!

*(We deal out all the remaining property, then play for a while, putting back properties we land on. We cheer when we land on something we own—and therefore can give back—and boo when we land on property our opponent owns.)*

*A:* Maybe we should give the other person the property when that happens? No, that would be too complicated.

*JB:* You'd like doing it all backward, but that would be changing it too much. You don't want to carry it too far.

*A:* It would be too confusing to change it too much.

*JB:* You're worried about making it too far from the way it's supposed to be.

*(We continue to play.)*

*JB:* Ooh—you only have two left. You've given everything else back? Wow! How did you get that far? Hm. It's funny to be glad you *don't* have any property. Usually that's a bad feeling, now it feels good to give away everything you own!

In my last comment, I was consciously thinking about Adena's giving away her clothes and wishing she could have them back. Again, my preference is not to say this directly, although I don't think it would be wrong to do that; I think it is more direct than I need to be—I can be useful without speaking in those terms—and could at times be prematurely direct or developmentally too advanced for a given child at a particular moment in treatment. I was thinking about Adena's outside life and trying to phrase my comment in a way that described both the game before us and Adena's world outside. She then had the choice of which aspect to respond to. She chose a simple grunt: "Yeah."

Soon after this session, Adena's parents came for their regular meeting with me. They reported that Adena enjoyed coming to therapy. They also reported some changes in her behavior. They noticed a little less fighting with her sister, fewer tears, easier bedtimes, and generally less obvious anxiety. I took this to mean that Adena's game playing with me was useful to her therapeutically; the ways she played Monopoly and other games were her expression of the concerns she had in the world, and the changes she made in the games were her attempts to show me more of her inner world, bring more of her difficulties into the therapy room and try out strategies she was afraid to use in the outside world.

Adena would never have cheated in real life; my pleasure at being with her when she did allowed her to feel that she might be likeable even if she did something against the rules. Her beating me and crossing me in the games she played allowed her to experiment with opposing her friends and relatives; she could see how she would feel as well as how I would react, without the long-term consequences of losing a friend or otherwise being punished. She could express all this freely in treatment, thereby feeling less anxiety over her need to do so outside of treatment, and gradually become both less inhibited from refusing people in her outside world and also less needy of doing so.

The interaction described above seemed to have been helpful enough to Adena, for she played in this give-back way only in that one session. She tested my willingness to play in whatever way struck her fancy, and she tried out the experience of taking away and giving back. I identified these feelings and played along; she seemed to need only one session of this sort, then went back to her usual method of following box-top rules more closely—buying property and trying to amass the most rather than the least. The helpfulness of this approach for Adena can be seen in the way she became less symptomatic at home while she played with me.

## LATER VARIATIONS

The next experiment with rule changing was of a different sort and lasted through several weeks:

> Months into treatment, Adena has regularly decided to start the game with all property dealt out at the start of the game. We then spend a few minutes trading: she offers me the last of my mostly owned monopolies and asks me for the last of hers. Over the weeks, she gradually tests asking to give me her utilities and railroads rather than requesting to keep them.
>
> In the first few games, she offers me every monopoly I partly own and carefully balances the trades: two or three cheaper properties for Boardwalk, two utilities for one rail-road. She proposes the lesser properties for herself. Over time she becomes braver in the trades she offers, asking to keep more for herself and refusing the trades she does not like.
>
> After we have traded each week, she—carefully and thoughtfully, as always—places hotels on her most valuable holdings. She holds on to enough cash to cover any expenses

she might incur. I do not, and she still begs me not to pay her the full amount when I land on Boardwalk.

In later sessions, to feel richer and to avoid my running out of money, she experiments with starting with more of the bank's money dealt to us at the beginning: we take five $500s one week, then 10, then we divide all of the bank's money between us, this while we continue to deal out all properties at the beginning of the game and spend the first few minutes trading for monopolies. We then spend much of our riches on hotels—I putting them with abandon everywhere and with all my money, Adena thoughtfully balancing what she spends with what she keeps on hand, developing only the most potentially lucrative of her holdings. When I run out of cash she asks me to owe it to her rather than mortgage properties.

Each week, Adena experiments with asserting herself more in the variant of the game she invents. She tests how much she can take my money and what she feels like when she does so. She puts herself in position to trounce me—by owning the most expensive property, putting hotels there for the highest income, and preserving her own assets more than I do—and then backs off from striking the fatal blow. I comment on this each time she plays, saying:

You're really set up to get me—that's a lot of money you'll get if I land there.

I didn't think I had enough money that time—I won't make it if I land there again. Even if I gave you all my ones, I don't think I would have enough money to pay that again.

Go to Jail, great! I'm safe from going bankrupt for a little while!

125

When she refuses my rent—she insists that I pay her all my $500s and most of my $100s but claims not to want "little money" at all—I describe this need: "You really don't want me to run out of money"; "You're trying to protect me from going bankrupt, even though I'm not doing a very good job of protecting myself." She agrees with my description and claims that she wants to keep playing, realizing that the game would be over if I ran out of assets. I say that I thought she might be worried about my feelings, too. She agrees: "I don't want anybody to hate me for winning." This is impressive insight Adena has expressed, gained from playing structured games creatively and applicable to many aspects of her life.

## A BIG CHANGE IN STYLE

In Adena's next alteration of the rules, we have transferred all of the bank's money (the money we have paid for hotels and that collected from taxes and Chance cards and the like) to the center of the board, to be won by the first player to land on Free Parking. We both circle the board several times, coming close but never landing on Free Parking. Adena plays the rest of the game as if it were inconsequential; she clearly cares only if she wins the grand lottery and not whether she gets or loses money any other way. She has even done away with collecting $200 at Go, offering a house as an optional substitution.

After five or six cycles I go to Jail, then get out with doubles. I throw again for my move and shoot two 5s—a perfect score to land on the grand prize of Free Parking—and still get an extra turn.

Adena grabs the Free Parking money before I can take it

and hides it under the table, simultaneously changing the 5s on my dice to 4s! Not only is there nothing left for me to win at Free Parking, but I land on her property instead!

Unable to maintain this stance, however, she hands me the money, turns the dice back to 10, and decides to put the game away for the end of our session.

This game represents a new development for Adena. She has altered the rules quite drastically for her, deciding how much money we will each get regardless of the box-top rules, redefining where the money should go, doing away with the Bank and even the quintessential $200 at Go. Contrary to her customary conservative play, in which she carefully plans and saves, she has created an enormous lottery in the center of the board. This is a winner-take-all adventure rather than her usual slow-but-steady-wins-the-race game.

Her strong conscience requires her to play fairly, waiting patiently for her ship to come in. Perhaps in time she would have miscounted her turn, but she did not in the span of this game. While she has always tried to protect me from major setbacks, this windfall is more than she can bear; she hides the prize and alters the dice. Her conscience wins out, though, and she undoes her actions. Adena's strengths are clear in this example: She wants this jackpot desperately and cannot bear that she has lost it, but she is able to play with stealing it back, to recognize that she is playing, and to restore the game to fair play. This is very close to the kind of ego strength observed in the children who are not in therapy, described in Chapter 4. The strain is still too much for Adena at that point, however, for she is not able to continue playing if she faces the loss she has just sustained. I mention this as well: "That hurt too much—it was *so* much money I just took, it made it no fun to play the game any more." I said this with a great deal of sympathy, for I never meant to be the one who won the jackpot. I expected Adena to find a way to get it for herself, I understood the pain of watching such a large prize disappear, I could imagine the hopelessness of trying to win after a loss like that, and I was truly impressed with Adena's ability to tolerate such a disappointment.


## FURTHER PROGRESS

After that game, Adena did not choose Monopoly for quite some time! Her progress continued to be visible in other games. I report one game of Life to show these developments:

Adena loves the game of Life and frequently chooses it for her play. She has almost always played according to her careful, thoughtful style—going to college, insuring her car and her home—and her considerate nature—worrying about my not making careful choices. I have deliberately played recklessly with her, never going to college or buying insurance, and often going into debt. (This was primarily to give Adena the experience of watching me play in a way that would worry her and to provide opportunities for her to allow me to suffer while she practiced not saving me. However, I must admit that I enjoyed flirting with board-game danger this way!)

This day, I won the toss to go first. I chose the career path and pulled the highest salary in my random draw. Adena watched this and changed her decision to go to college—a progressive ability to change her mind and to not worry about the safety of college choices. She announced, "I'm going to pick $20,000 [salary] on purpose, so I can trade with you on a 'trade salaries with another player' space."

She did not pick the $20,000 salary—perhaps because it seemed too extreme a sacrifice—but pulled a card at random, ending up with $60,000, still significantly lower than my $100,000. We played properly for a while.

Adena came to the first "trade salaries" space. She threw the dice, threw a number close to but not exactly the number she needed to land on it, and miscounted her move so that she landed there. She eagerly traded with me, gleefully leaving me with the lower salary, and pointed that out to me every time either of us landed on Payday for the rest of the game. When I landed on a "trade salaries" space later in the game, she told me I had miscounted and recreated my move for me to be sure I landed on a different square!

This game of Life is an exquisite example of Adena's successful response to treatment. When she began her work with me she was self-destructively overconsiderate of her acquaintances, and she showed this in the way she played board games with me. She played competitively but conservatively, staying just slightly ahead of me in her games, protecting me from suffering too many setbacks or losing by too much. In this Life game, she was able to try her luck without a safety net and to win at my expense. She won handily, taking my money to do it, and was able to express her undisguised delight at doing so.

In learning to "cheat" at board games, Adena has not learned to cheat in real life; rather, she has used board-game play to try out new behaviors, to discover how she feels about not following rules precisely, or asking for what she wants, or winning against another person. The cheating does not extend to her life outside therapy, but her newly gained insight does, as does her newfound ability to ask for what she wants from others.


## CONCLUSION

In this nearly 1 year of treatment shown primarily on the Monopoly board, Adena grew from a child who worried about the feelings of everyone but herself to one who could safeguard her own interests. Her board-game play demonstrated this progress in the way she started by protecting me from her taking too much of my assets, developed through stages of testing out various methods of taking away and giving back as well as ways to make my game suffer, and culminated in her taking my money directly away for her own purposes while expressing her glee at doing so.

Shortly after this last game, she reported that she had found the strength to confront the offender in her class and demand her favorite hat back. Thus, in board-game play Adena expressed her needs and fears and tried out alternative ways of being, while I described her experiences and helped her do to me, metaphorically, what she wished to do to her friends. This resulted in her being able to behave more successfully in her outside life.

# CHAPTER EIGHT

# *I* Hate *This Game.* . . .
# *The Therapist's Experience of Board Games*

My brothers used to play Monopoly with me. They were all
older and much wiser than I. They would advise me whenever
there was a choice to be made—whether to buy a property or
when to put houses on it or pay my way out of Jail—but they
always advised me of what would be good for *them*. They would
tell me not to buy Boardwalk, then one of them would buy it
and right away put houses on it when I was coming around the
board. They didn't seem to care which one of them won—it
was just great sport to watch me lose. But losing wasn't enough;
they had to play until I was completely bankrupt, and the game
had to end with me in tears. So now, whenever Gregory takes
out the Monopoly game, I cringe. I don't seem to be over this,
even now.

This was a story told to me by an adult, long past worrying about
her brothers' cruelty, who found that her early experiences with

131

Monopoly had colored her current feelings about it. She understood the irrationality of her cringing (and she prides herself on being a highly rational person), but could not control it.

## HISTORIES OF BOARD GAMES

When I was a little boy I used to need to win, or I would cry, and my parents could not bear such display of emotion. So they discussed this and decided that my father should play with me and teach me how to lose. He spent hours with me—playing checkers, Parcheesi, basketball, running races, everything—and beat me at every one, over and over until I could lose without crying.

I'm really lucky—it's not anything I do, it just seems to happen. When I play cards I get fantastic hands more than other people; when I play a game where you need to win by exact count, I get the count. So I like playing games a lot, even now. But other people don't seem to like them as much—or at least don't want to play as much as I do. I could get together with friends and play all night and into the morning, but other people aren't willing to keep going like that.

Everyone has a history of game play and experiences of competition, winning, and losing. When friends and colleagues discuss board games, almost everyone has a story to tell: the way one person's older brothers used to tromp her at Monopoly, making her hate Monopoly forever. Or the way another's father set about to play every game in his repertoire, and to beat him in order to teach him a lesson about winning and losing. Or the way another felt driven to read books on better strategies so that he could return to his usual play opponent with new methods of winning by a landslide. Or the memory of no one being willing to play with another because she had such a natural talent for games that she won too often against would-be friends. Or the pain of the pressure from parents to play better, the tears of younger siblings, the gloating of an older cousin.

These histories, of course, affect the way we are able to play with child patients and have to be considered. I suggested to the Monopoly phobe, for instance, that she remove that game from the room, because it continued to raise anxiety in her. Interestingly, she reported that after she talked about Monopoly with me, she no longer felt the same repulsion.

This is the classic understanding of countertransference reactions: countertransference comes from difficulties in our own childhood and disappears when we understand and analyze it. There is a great deal of value in that approach to our experiences as therapists. We should be aware of our feelings about the work that we do and attempt to understand where it comes from and what it leads to. Some of our feelings are rooted in our childhoods, some are not; some are caused by and lead to blocks or difficulties of some sort, some not.

## RESOLVING OUR OWN DIFFICULTIES

I think one difficulty that a number of child therapists have with board games stems from their training in child therapy, rather than from their childhood experiences. I was taught from the literature and by my supervisors that board games were not useful in child

therapy. Games could be offered to difficult children as an entice-
ment to attend therapy if absolutely necessary, but we should try to
move children away from structured games into more productive
pursuits. We could offer action figures, puppets, dollhouses. We
could try to discuss the child's life. We could at least use therapeutic
board games. But we should never play checkers—at least not
willingly. That left me with a terrible dilemma, one that I have heard
other therapists describe as well: Latency-age patients want to play
checkers, but we believe that we are not supposed to. We then have
our choice of refusing to accommodate our patients' needs, refusing
to accommodate our supervisors' wishes, or guiltily playing checkers
while wishing we could stop.

There is a similar dilemma posed by the cheating that seems
ubiquitous in child psychotherapy. We "know" from our early
teachings that cheating is wrong, and we believe we ought to be good
role models helping children acquire appropriate life patterns. And
we are taught (Bixler, 1949; Ginott, 1959; Ginott and Lebo, 1962)
about the importance of setting limits with the children we work
with. But we are uncomfortable criticizing or controlling our patients' play, because this is so foreign to the way we handle all other
playroom interactions. So therapists tell me they pretend not to see
the child's cheating, or they silently give a little grin when they
notice it, feeling guilty that their response does not set adequate
limits. Or else they do confront the child's cheating, feeling guilty
that their response is not therapeutic.

I have found that the concepts I have described have helped
some of the therapists I have spoken to in breaking through these
guilty feelings, and I hope they will help future readers of this book
as well. If we understand that structured game playing is a common
expectable stage of development, we may feel less that it does not

belong in the treatment of children at that stage, and we can then play free of guilt. If we reconceptualize cheating as creative play and see it as expressive and therefore helpful in the therapeutic process rather than harmful, we may feel able to observe it free of guilt.

Similarly, I have found that therapists' feelings of competitiveness are sometimes based on their training as child therapists rather than their own childhood experiences. If we are fully playing the board game as a game, and if we are responsible for controlling the cheating so that a "fair" game can occur, then we must also play our best to win. We try not to lie to children about other aspects of the treatment, or to keep secrets from them. Playing less than competitively would be keeping our full abilities secret, lying about them. When games in psychotherapy are seen as metaphoric expressions of a child's dynamics, our own competitiveness—our own playing—becomes irrelevant. I find that when I focus on my curiosity on what makes a child cheat, when and how it begins, and what it reveals about the child's life and unconscious, I do not generally think about my performance in the game. When I occasionally find myself concerned with my own performance, I can use this information in the treatment. If we are always competitive, we should examine ourselves and work with this constriction in our own therapy. If we are generally free from competitive feelings toward the children we work with but occasionally experience some, we can use this important information in aid of that child's treatment.

## PATTERNS OF IMPEDENCES

There are some occasions when our own concerns do regularly impede our therapeutic abilities. I try to monitor the patterns on these occasions in myself so that I can understand or control the circumstances that raise my own feelings to a nontherapeutic level with the children I see. I also limit the materials available in my playroom to those with which I feel comfortable playing.

> Scott likes basketball; he is consumed with it. He knows all the players and the standing of all the teams, both college and professional. He plays—alone—in his spare time. In treatment he can only recite basketball plays and fidget uncomfortably in his seat. I finally suggest that we play together because he seems interested in nothing else. For our next session, I bring a basketball and change into play clothes before Scott's session. We go outside to a basketball net that is left over from a previous use of the facility grounds. We play, hard and fast. While I play, I notice Scott's play. He is strong and agile, with natural ability but little control. He pushes hard but ineffectively.
>
> Over the next few months, Scott's play improves. As I discuss his moves, he also notices his ineffectuality. We talk about his impulsive need to grab the ball rather than wait for an opening. We recognize the waxing and waning of his aggressiveness—strong when he has had a bad day or a bad week at school—and his proficiency—better when he remains calm and thoughtful and in control of his emotions. (E. Tuccillo, personal communication, 1977)

This is an example of sports play used as a structured board game might be. The therapist uses Scott's style of play and his rule-breaking patterns (here, committing fouls) as material for interpretation and discussion. The therapy proceeds within the metaphor of the game—here basketball rather than checkers or Sorry, but in the same way that I have advocated for play on a game board.

It is not my example.

I find I have difficulty playing gross motor activity games like basketball or other sports. I think sports can be used exactly like the other structured games I have described here, and have been by many (cf., e.g., Altman, 1997; Shaw, 1998). I cannot use them, though, because I cannot focus enough on a child's dynamics—because of my own need to perform well, or the danger I feel to my self-esteem when I do not, or the amount of energy and intensity I use to play physically, which drains my ability to attend to the therapy I am supposed to be performing. If I had been the therapist in the above example, I might have been able to serve Scott as an adequate basketball partner, or I might have concentrated on his dynamics and discussed the way he was playing, but I do not think I would have been able to do both, as his therapist did. In any case, I have too much difficulty with physical play to be able to use it therapeutically, so I do not have balls and racquets and such on my shelves, and I would not have suggested to Scott that we play. Children who find it important to play ball often make materials or bring their own.

We should not have games available if we hate them, or if we love them, either, or hold masters' credentials, because any of these make it difficult for us to listen to the child's experience of the game rather than our own. It is important to monitor our own responses to various games in this way, and to pay attention to them in the choices we make for the playroom, to make ourselves able to be productive therapists.

My preferences are for games of luck rather than skill. I can live with my own bad luck more easily than my own inabilities to play well. When a child manipulates dice or miscounts moves, I can easily discuss the child's dynamics without even being tempted to win. So I fill my shelves with games that children like and that have at least some component of luck involved: Candyland, cards, Sorry, Chutes and Ladders, Life. Chess—a game entirely of skill—is not my preference, so I provide it only when a child like Richard (Chapter 1) has specifically requested it. Connect Four is also a game of skill that I do not care for. I have played it when I have used space others share, so the game has already been in the room, but I prefer not to provide it in my office.

The exceptions, of course, are games of skill that I like. I enjoy puzzles and tangrams, and I can usually participate in them in such a way that leaves me free to think about my patient's dynamics, or wait while they find a piece for themselves, or understand rather than resent it when they undo my work for being "wrong."

Our responsibility is to examine our experiences to uncover and resolve conflicts from our own childhoods that interfere with our ability to play therapeutically with children in treatment with us, and choose games that will be both interesting to children and comfortable for us. We should analyze our blind spots so they do not impede us, and we should remove Monopoly or basketball if they will not allow us to perform therapeutically while we play.

## MONITORING OUR REACTIONS

Once the games available are edited to be games that we can play comfortably and with interest primarily in our patient's patterns, we can monitor our reactions with individual patients. If we are generally not competitive but feel it with one child or in one game, that becomes important information about our work in that session.

138

Harvey is playing Mastermind. He is the "master," I the "mind," trying to guess his code. It is hard for him to wait for me to think or to guess incorrectly; he tells me which of my guesses is correct and which is not. Then I create a code, and he guesses. He is surprisingly good, making what seem to be very lucky guesses very quickly and cracking the code accurately within four or five trials. As he leaves the office at the end of the session he says, "You know, you can cheat at that game really easy." "Did you cheat?" I ask. "Yes," he says, "I looked while you were making up your pattern." And he walks out the door.

This is an example cited in Chapter 4. It is repeated here to discuss an additional aspect of the session: I was writing a book on cheating while I was working with Harvey, but I did not notice his peeking! This tells me something important about my interactions with Harvey. Why did I fail to notice this common method of cheating? Why did I fail to question his rapid code breaking? Why did I ignore my knowledge that he is an anxious child who cannot usually calmly think through a complex problem like a Mastermind code? What made me believe he could guess correctly after only one or two trials, repeatedly, by honest luck?

The answers to these questions are complex. My feelings about Mastermind are partly to blame, because it is a game I enjoy and—obviously—get wrapped up in. My first clue to my own difficulties should have been my annoyance with Harvey when he told me his code rather than let me enjoy guessing. I wanted this game to be a fair one, so I ignored the evidence that it was not. I was playing the game, not serving as Harvey's therapist.

My feelings about Harvey are also evident. He is a tall, quiet boy who appears 2 or 3 years older than his actual age, which is already a year or so beyond his regressed emotional state. He has suffered throughout his life from being treated as more mature than he could be, and I fell into that same trap. He seemed to protect this misperception here, surreptitiously peeking rather than cheating more blatantly. My previous relationship with him—or maybe just my dumb luck—was strong enough that Harvey could admit his sins as he left the room, helping me with his therapy process.

## ANOTHER EXAMPLE

Abigail and I are playing Monopoly, have been for most of the hour and for most of the previous hours. She manipulates the game so that she wins by extraordinary good "luck" repeatedly. She "tosses" doubles twice on every turn. She "lands" on all the expensive properties and everything she needs to complete her monopolies. She "wins" free parking money when the kitty is very full (of the money I have paid in!). In this particular game I have a few monopolies, and I have placed hotels on one whole side of the board. Suddenly, I look up and notice that it is 3 minutes past the time to end our session. Not only have I failed to give my usual 5-minute warning, I have failed to notice time to clean up or end our session either.

Once again, this is an example of a time when interactions with a child created reactions different from my usual experiences. I routinely give 5-minute warnings to children I work with; why did I miss it this time? I often miss by a minute or 2—but almost never miss the warning altogether. With Abigail, especially, the warning had represented an important opportunity to work on her feelings about separation each week. I routinely put games away and clean the playroom before children leave their sessions so that they have the opportunity to watch me restore order to whatever chaos they may have created during their hour. Abigail left little to clean up, but what made me fail to follow my usual procedures?

In this case, I believe it was my experience with Abigail rather than my feelings about the game we were playing. She is a child who creates a brightly optimistic front for the world and for herself, and I had been interpreting her need to feel positive about everything, to no avail. While the end of every session regularly represented a setback for her, we had not made headway in understanding or altering her character in the few minutes we had had to think about this each week. In the game, however, we had a prime opportunity—or we would have, if we could have played a little longer. Abigail had allowed me more success in this game than she usually does, possibly due to the progress we had made in her treatment, possibly due to the excesses of "luck" she had provided for herself. I owned two monopolies, strategically placed on one leg of the board. It was clear that it would be difficult for her to avoid landing on one of my properties for long, because the only other options on that side of the board were opportunities to lose money through taxes or Chance cards. I was unconsciously hoping that I could make the session last long enough for her to experience the disappointment of one of these minor losses to me so that we would have the opportunity to observe and discuss her reaction.

Three minutes overtime—actually 8 minutes, because I usually start the process 5 minutes before the end of the hour—may not seem like very much time. For Abigail, however, it had been an important part of her learning to trust me, because I would predictably warn her before she would have to lose me each week, and I demonstrated that I would never lose control of time. No matter how frightening the material we dealt with might become to her, I would always be able to stop us and help her rejoin the outside world. I was there to work hard to help her deal with her anxieties. So my losing track of time represented an act that could scare her—out of complacency and into expressing some of the negative feelings I was sure she must be hiding from.

## CONCLUSION

We should monitor our own needs, to compete or to concentrate on the game or to finish before the time is up. When we have powerful needs ourselves, we may have difficulty using games in treatment, lest we try to control the child's play in our own interests rather than the child's. In my own case, I try to concentrate on questions about what dynamics are being revealed, which usually seems to block most of my own needs in the game. I resign myself to losing—not *making* myself lose, but expecting that the Harvey's and Abigail's I work with will cheat and so they will win instead of me—perhaps in defense against my own fear of losing. Of course, this also prevents me from feeling that my own self-esteem is on the line: I am not playing to win, so I have not really lost. I especially do not have to face the feeling of failure in losing to a 9-year-old! My performance in games should be irrelevant during a session, because I use structured games like any other grist for the mill.

Then my own experience with games changes because of my history with the children I see in treatment. I enjoy games vicariously because of the children's enjoyment, and I find them useful because children reveal themselves to me through them. When I have an unusual response—annoyance, for example, or impatience or competitiveness—or I lose track of the time or forget the patient's dynamics, I can use that information also as grist for the mill, as indications of what is revealed about the two of us and the therapeutic process.

# CHAPTER NINE

# Groupies:
# The Uses of Board Games in Group Therapy

It is Friday afternoon. A group of four second-graders is playing Sorry in the resource room, as a fun way to reinforce math and reading skills and as reward for a week of hard work. Alex, whose counting skills are the weakest of the group, does not always count his moves accurately; the teacher is conflicted over whether to call him on this or whether to allow him his uninterrupted fun. Believing he is not intentionally miscounting most of the time, she decides to let him be most of the time, challenging his count only rarely. She is similarly conflicted about Michael's moves; however, because he is able to count more accurately than Alex, she tends to challenge Michael more frequently. Neither of these positions is fully comfortable for her.

Alex moves eight spaces on a 7 roll; it happens that this lands him on Leroy's square, thus sending Leroy back to Start. The teacher, again uncertain of Alex's intent and therefore unsure of the appropriate response from her, says nothing. Leroy, however, screams, "Hey! That's not where you are. You've been cheating this whole game. Make him stop cheating, Ms. Sullivan!"

This is representative of the kind of interaction often described to me by professionals who work with groups of children using board games: Children in groups stretch rules, just as children in individual therapy do, and their therapists are unsure of how to respond. The approach recommended for individual therapy in this book— allowing the child to play in his own way and watching for dynamics that can be understood and interpreted—is more complicated with groups because other children are present. Their needs—having a partner who plays fairly—are at odds with their play, creating new rules of their own.

The example demonstrates the difficulties of playing structured board games with groups of children. The rest of this book has described methods of play in which the therapist—in the interest of understanding and aiding children in their struggle with learning and accepting rules—allows them to alter and stretch box-top rules until they resolve their conflicts and become able to play fairly.

In group treatment, however, there are other children present, children who are struggling with their own conflicts over rules and fair play. They are unable to use the box-top rules but angry at the other children who cheat. The therapist has the option of allowing all children to change rules—thus appearing to encourage cheating—or enforcing rules for all children—thus playing police officer throughout the session, offering little of therapeutic benefit to the children and feeling frustrated and exhausted herself. This is especially difficult for teachers, like Ms. Sullivan in the group above, who feel they cannot allow cheating in their charges but worry about contributing to low self-esteem if they are too critical.

For these reasons, I think board games should not be used as board games with children in groups. One can allow them to play on their own, like the children playing Sorry in Chapter 4, intervening only when called in and offering only dire consequences (confiscation of the game, for example) in the event of egregious misconduct. Other than that, I have not found that the structure of board games lends itself well to the needs of children in groups.

This does not mean that games are useless for groups. Games where everybody plays and nobody wins are excellent activities for children's groups, and therapeutic games designed to elicit projective material are especially useful.

I have written elsewhere (Bellinson, 1991) about using games with children in psychiatric hospitals. Here, I would like to advocate using games—or at least aspects of them—with groups of children in other settings as well. Games for children's groups provide activities that are interesting and enjoyable, while helping children identify and express thoughts and feelings.

Traditional group therapy for children (Corder, 1986; Ginott, 1961; Meeks, 1977; Rachman, 1977; Sands & Golub, 1977; Scheidlinger & Rauch, 1972; Siepker & Kandaras, 1985; Slavson, 1943, 1955; Slavson & Schiffer, 1975; Sugar, 1974; Van Scoy, 1971, 1977) does not recommend structured games. These groups tend to be play therapy groups for young children or activity group therapy for latency-age and preadolescent children. In these groups, children play without direction from the group leader, who watches and uses the information he observes to formulate his therapeutic approach.

However, most of these authors explicitly state that they believe such groups are not appropriate for severely disturbed children and children with poor reality testing, inadequate impulse control, or a history of severe emotional deprivation beginning in early infancy. Slavson (1943, 1955; Slavson & Schiffer, 1975) states that activity group therapy is effective only insofar as members are selected carefully and groups are balanced properly. He claims that children who are narcissistic, sadistic, punishment seeking, homosexual, extremely aggressive, acting out by theft or homicidal behavior, psychotic or otherwise severely disturbed, psychopathic, mentally deficient, or lacking a minimum level of ego function, superego function, or object-relating capacity are inaccessible to activity group therapy. Even learning-disabled children were thought to be unreachable by traditional group therapy techniques.

It is my experience that children in treatment with none of these contraindicated difficulties are rare; a group full of them would be hard to come by. My experience with children in psychiatric hospitals and day treatment centers, though, has taught me that children who are too disturbed or otherwise unsuitable for traditional groups can still make productive group members and can still make use of group therapy. In a previous paper (Bellinson, 1991), I described games to play to make group techniques applicable to an inpatient unit; here, I would like to discuss more of these games to use with children at any psychological level.

Latency-age children play structured games. This is true of children at all levels of adjustment, individually and in groups. For individual treatment to be successful, children have to enjoy participating. Thus, we offer dramatic play and board games to make their treatment interesting to them, and we learn to interpret their play to make their treatment therapeutic. The same might be said of group treatment: We should offer games to make the group interesting to children, and we should learn to understand their play to make the group therapeutic.

The boards of board games, however, do not seem to do this. The boards turn the focus of the game toward progression around the course, who is ahead and who is behind, and thoughts of rule bending to make each child win. In individual treatment this focus is acceptable, because the therapist can help the child with these important issues, because the therapist, presumably, has a focus other than winning. In a group, however, all the participants might be focused on winning and cheating; the therapist can be stuck serving only as referee.

The group itself supports participation in these games, and the therapist can facilitate play and help understand the meaning of the material that emerges. There is enough structure in the group itself—rules about where to sit, when to talk, how to listen, and what subject to focus on—that latency-age children can still work out their developmental issues and difficulties with structure in the group, without a specific board game to play.

Beyond that, there are ways to play games that do not involve a board or winning and losing that serve well. Expressive games and games without boards to measure progress or rewards for successes or identification of winners and losers are ideal for group therapy.


## GAMES FOR CHILDREN'S GROUPS

The Talking, Feeling and Doing Game, for instance, when played without a game board, can be a way to evoke information about the lives and psychological states of the group members, both individually and as a group.

I leave the board, spinner, and chips hidden away, and bring only a stack of cards, all colors shuffled together. I try to choose a variety of cards at several levels of emotional arousal, leaving out cards that refer to turns: win a turn, lose a turn, move ahead three spaces. Group members choose a card at random (although most of them know which are the talking, which are the feeling, and which are the doing cards, and choose according to their own preference), read it or have it read for them, and perform the assignment. If a member does not want to participate she does not have to. If she cannot think of a response, after we allow time and encouragement for her to think, I ask other group members to offer their response, then return to the card picker to ask again. After one child has responded I offer others the option of discussing the response and/or offering their own response. The group can then compare notes on the best parts of each of their mothers, their feelings about a boy who expels gas, their pantomimes of their respective bad dreams. When we have discussed all of each card that we can productively, I ask for a new volunteer to choose another card.

Francine, a child from foster care in a girl's group, chooses a Talking card: Say something bad about your mother. The group groans. Francine seems frozen. I know Francine's mother is anything but perfect, and that part of Francine's difficulties are caused by her inability to acknowledge this even to herself. I therefore prompt her: "I really, really love my mother, but. . . ." She still stands, paralyzed. "Try," I say, "I really, really, really, really, *really* love my mother, but sometimes she . . ." Francine haltingly says, "I really, really, really, really,

really love my mother, but sometimes she doesn't visit me enough," and she runs to her seat to sit down and hide there. "Wow," I say, "that was hard to do—to say something bad about somebody you love so much. It was pretty scary. I bet lots of people here would feel bad to say something bad about their mothers." And the group joins in a rousing, "Yeah!" Ellen follows: "It gives me the creeps just to think it!"

*Jasmine:* I know what you mean.
*Julie:* Yeah. I get like pins and needles all over my skin.
*Natalie:* Sometimes I get afraid that she'll know if I say something like that, and then she'll get really mad at me.
*Ellen:* Word! (an expression that means wholehearted agreement) And then she'll be even worse than whatever I just said was bad about her.
*JB:* So it sounds like everybody's mom has some bad things about her, and everybody's a little scared to think about those bad things.
*Stephanie:* Yeah, now it's my turn to pick a card.

In this example, the Feeling card chosen allowed Francine to consider her conflicted feelings about her consciously beloved mother, briefly. In individual treatment I might have focused on this further, but in the group I chose not to dwell on that aspect of the experience. I felt that it could have been too painful for a fragile child like Francine and that it might have left her exposed to group scrutiny and scorn for criticizing her mother. On the other hand, her fear of expressing herself seemed very close to her consciousness, quite available for discussion, and the group's groan suggested to me that other members also sympathized with Francine's predicament.

Their support for her difficulties and their elaboration of the conflict helped her feel understood, part of the shared whole, and better able to think further about her feelings in future discussions.

Others techniques of Gardner's approaches to resistant children (1971, 1973, 1975) are also useful with groups of children, as are variations of those approaches.

## BAG OF THINGS GAME

Using Gardner's suggestions, I have created a Bag of Things, holding a variety of objects such as a baby bottle, a photograph in a small frame, a Band-Aid box, a shoelace, a rubber dagger, and so on. I also always include a package of candy—chewing gum, M&M's, Starburst—holding enough for each group member to have a small piece (as well as tell a story about it) if anyone picks it out of the bag. Children reach into the bag at random, "no feeling around for something else" (although that stops the process about as much as box-top rules stop cheating!), to choose an object to tell a story about. Here, again, I do not use the chips that Gardner recommends for individual treatment. Group pressure is sufficient to ensure that children want to participate, either by telling a story or by expanding on someone else's; chips only add the rivalry of winning or losing to an otherwise supportive exploratory process. Children's stories express their psychological themes, both individually and as a group.

> One child in one group playing the Bag of Things game chose the baby bottle. She told of a new mother, delighted to have an adorable baby. She was warming the bottle to feed her infant, after which she would bathe the baby and get it all dressed up

and ready to go out. It was going to Grandma's house, where all the relatives would gather to see the newborn and offer the mother gifts.

Another group playing the same game was about to lose one of the group leaders. The child picking the baby bottle told of a mother who was out of milk, uncertain of whether to let the baby go hungry or leave the baby alone while she went out to the grocery store.

These are two stories about the same object in two different groups of girls at about the same age. The first story is one full of pleasure—a new baby, a delighted mother, relatives bearing gifts. The second group not only could not imagine a happy life with a baby, the storyteller could not even think of a way to take her baby to the grocery store with her! Life for the second group member was desolate, full of hardship and deprivation. If the group leader was leaving, this group member could conceive of no nurturance anywhere in the world.

My comments in these groups centered on describing the experiences of the child telling the stories. In the first, I talked of her delight at having a baby, what good care she was taking of it, and how nice it was to have so many relatives be so pleased with it. I also asked if it was good or bad to have the baby be the center of attention—if all the gifts were for the baby, the mother might feel left out. I asked the rest of the group to join the discussion, and they were able to describe additional feelings of envy, jealousy, exhaustion, loneliness, and deprivation, which might accompany feelings of delight at having a new baby. My goal was to help the group see past the first-glance delight of a newborn to the myriad of feelings

153

that always accompany parenthood, without denying them the fantasy of pleasures that they imagined for themselves when they gave birth.

In the second group above, I talked of the pain in the dilemma—that this poor mother could see no possible way out: the baby was going to be deprived one way or another, either of her milk or her mother. It was terrible for the baby and terrible for the mother as well, because the mother probably wanted her baby to feel good and not hungry. My emphasis was on the mother's inability to see a solution—not that there actually *was* no solution; it was most striking to me that it did not occur to the storyteller to take the baby to the store with her. I then continued to talk about the pain of loss in more general terms. I said the baby must feel very empty, that she needed somebody to take better care of her since she could not take care of herself, that she could not even say what she needed but relied on someone else to know what she needed and provide it, that she must be very scared that no one understood and no one was there to take care of her, and maybe she was angry as well. I mentioned that the mother did not mean to hurt her baby that way, but that that did not matter to the baby, who was equally hurt whether her mother meant it or not. My goal here was to help the group, in their identification with the baby of the storyteller, to fully feel their own pain at the loss of their nurturing group leader. My thoughts were of the group's feelings about their pending loss; my words were general statements about loss of any sort. They applied equally to the milk-deprived baby, the leader-deprived group members, and the past deprivations the members had suffered in their own lives.

This group went on to talk a bit about their own deprivations, starting with one girl who agreed, "Yeah, nobody ever understands us, either. We have a lot of needs, but everybody just thinks we're strong and angry and we should be punished. We're like babies in some ways, too." The other members concurred, and went on to talk about their mothers abandoning them, their teachers screaming at them, their peers fighting them. I briefly referred to the current situation, saying, "And here you are in a group where you're supposed to be getting help, and we're abandoning you and not understanding you, too." The members concurred and added it to their list of offenses by the world against them.


## BOX OF WORDS GAME

Also following Gardner (1973), I have created a Box of Words. For my own interest, I have a different container for each of my games—a Bag of Things, a Box of Words, a Pitcher of Feelings, and so on—so when I enter a group holding one of them, the group instantly recognizes the game we will be playing.

The box contains words similar to the objects described above: Baby Bottle, Photograph, Band-Aids, Bad Dream, Ice Cream Cone, Pizza, Broken Leg, and so on, written on small pieces of paper and stored in a box. Children choose a word and tell whatever story occurs to them. Other children can add to the story or choose a new word. Groups can discuss other children's responses, compare them, and begin to understand their meaning.


## PITCHER OF FEELINGS GAME

The Pitcher of Feelings is my own invention, after the model of Gardner's games. I have a variety of feelings—sad, angry, happy, joyful, loving, loved, sexy, depressed, and so on—written on pieces of colored paper. (Feelings seemed to me to call for colors rather than white paper.) Children pick a feeling out of the pitcher and take their turn.

Sometimes the chooser acts out a time when he felt the feeling he has picked. Interestingly, children often find that it is difficult to portray a feeling alone; their experiences seem to be of feelings as responsive to someone else. So they often pick a partner to enact the emotion with them. The group discusses the feeling and the circumstances inducing it, when they have had the same feeling, and what aroused it in them. We also talk about what they do when they feel the emotion: Do they find a way to rid themselves of uncomfortable feelings? Try to hold on to pleasant ones? Do group members share these traits or differ from each other? These discussions work better for late-latency and early adolescent children. Younger children can act out what they might do about the feeling rather than talk about it.

> One very explosive, impulsive boy picks a red card that says "angry." He has a friend join him; they whisper briefly, then the second child pantomimes, grabbing the red card away from the first. The first puffs up, makes a fist, pretends to hit the second, and kicks—hard—at a metal cabinet in the therapy room. The group jumps as we are all startled at the unexpected clamor of the kick to the metal. I laugh and say, "So that makes you angry, when somebody takes something that belongs to you." "Yes," says the first actor, and there is assent from the rest of the group as well. "And then," I say, "you kick something?" Assent again. A member of the group pipes up,

"But that doesn't help—it just hurts your foot!" "Yeah," says the kicker, "I really hurt myself that time, and I was just playing!" Another boy says, "But you're not allowed to kick the person who did it!" The group agrees, "Yeah, then they send you here [to group]!" I offer, "You feel like kicking the person who did it, and you feel like you have to kick *something*." One boy suggests that if he doesn't kick something, he holds on to the feeling much longer, that kicking—or punching or hitting—helps the feeling go away. "Hm," I say, "but then you hurt your foot, or you get into trouble for kicking somebody. It seems like once you feel angry, there's not going to be an end until something bad happens to you." There is general agreement that angry feelings always end in unpleasantness. "So do you think you should never get angry?" I say: "*Could* you never get angry?" Some children think that would be possible, some do not. We wonder about this for a while, until one boy claims he wants a turn at picking another card.

Sometimes we play a guessing game with the Pitcher of Feelings: the chooser has to act out the feeling so that the rest of us can guess what it is. Again, this often requires a partner. It also seems to require a number of skills that deeply troubled children may not possess: discriminating one feeling from another—sadness as opposed to anger, for example; displaying feelings differentially—being angry should look different from being depressed; separating oneself from the play—acting out the feeling of anger without actually feeling angry. This game also seems to be more successful with older children and adolescents.

## CHARADES

Charades, or role playing, is an excellent game to play with groups of children. Young children and girls of all ages enjoy it. I play it as a group activity rather than a structured game. There are no teams chosen, no points assigned. One child or more acts out the charade, and the rest of the group watches, guesses, and discusses. Assignments can be written down and placed in a hat, or they can be assigned verbally by the group leader if she can think fast enough or prepare ideas beforehand.

While pantomiming and guessing can be fun for the children, I often prefer role playing rather than strict charades. Then children are not restricted to silence, and there are opportunities for more complex expression and discussion. Assignments include experiences children are likely to identify with:

Your mother has just baked a cake and gone out. The cake is sitting on the kitchen table, smelling *Delicious*—and you are starving. You wonder if you can take a piece and get your brother blamed for it.

You are taking a test and the teacher calls your name and claims you were cheating.

Your best friend just came to your house and told you her parents were going to get a divorce.

You are walking down the street when a stranger walks up to you and says hello.

You won the lottery!

Children play out the role they have been assigned. Then I ask what it felt like to play the various parts, what observers felt like watching, the probability that the event would unfold the way it was portrayed, whether other members have had similar experiences, and so on. Often the discussion leads to further role playing on the same topic. Other children want to display their version of the same events, or even add to the end of the story begun by the first child.

> One group of girls on an inpatient unit who were dealing with a new, strong authority on the unit played the scene where one of them was accused of cheating. The two players—the teacher and the alleged cheater—asked a third to play a student whose paper was or was not copied from. The student and teacher argued. The teacher called the principal, who called the police, who called the judge.

Discussion after this long, involved role play centered on the experiences of the players. As I asked each child what it felt like to play her part, the Teacher and Principal said they felt for the first time the frustration of their own teachers at trying to break through their own oppositional natures. The police and judge described the flattery of being considered higher authorities. The observers all had ideas for each role about other ways to handle the situation—which they also acted out. Each group member seems to have benefited from this active role playing.

To begin and end a group gently, first and last role assignments should be emotionally neutral or pleasant, and can include such portrayals as winning the lottery, walking a dog, reading a funny book, meeting an old friend on the street, scoring in soccer or basketball, or passing a test in school. Mid-group roles can involve

159

more anxiety-arousing issues as reading a pornographic book, missing a score in soccer or basketball, failing a test, dealing with a bully, or thinking about shoplifting. Other roles can be assigned to address the issues of one child or the whole group.

If the group leaders assign roles to be played out, charades can be tailor-made for each group and for each group participant. These roles can be planned in advance so that the therapist does not have to create ideas on the spot, and so that she has a number of possibilities ready for each meeting.

I came upon Gertie, a young preadolescent girl, at the candy store before a group meeting. She was a large girl who appeared much older than her 12 years, and one of the salespeople was flirting with her quite actively. She seemed unclear of the meaning of his communications but giggled and walked silently away.

In group later, Gertie asked to take a turn. I suggested, "You are sitting on a bench on the street, minding your own business, when a guy comes along and tries to ask you out." Gertie asked for a partner to be the guy; the rest of the girls refused to pretend to be boys, but they all offered whistles and catcalls for Gertie to respond to. She played for several minutes before she screamed, "Hey, this is just like the guy at the candy store!" and laughed. She then directed the other girls to say and do what the salesman had, and she rehearsed responses like, "I'm only twelve years old, you know," "Thanks, but I'll just take bubble gum please," and "Are you some kind of a pervert?!" The group agreed that they also felt confused when someone approached them in this way and offered additional suggestions for refusing or even accepting advances.

At other times, roles can be created to meet the needs of a group as a whole. A newly formed group can act out meeting new classmates. An ending group can act out a bon voyage. A group of disabled children can act out people staring unkindly. A group of children in foster care can act out reunions, both pleasant and disastrous, with biological parents. Then the members can be asked about their experiences, acting in the role play, watching the role play, or in life outside the group.

## OTHER ACTIVITIES

The goal of a group leader is to foster interaction among group members so that they can communicate with, understand, and help each other. Almost anything can serve as stimulation for group interaction. Photographs, movies, television shows, or popular songs raise issues that can be used as the beginning of discourse. Themes of Anger, Death, or Three Wishes can be presented by the therapist for group conversation.

Construction materials are usually of interest to latency-age children. These can include crayons, clay, collage materials, tongue depressors and glue, Lincoln Logs, and so on. These can serve as group activities if there is only one type of material provided per session, there is a group table or floor area provided for all children to congregate if they wish, the therapist listens for and structures group discussion while construction occurs, and children are encouraged to work together if they wish. For instance, paper for drawing can be a large long roll rather than individual pieces. That way children can stretch out on the floor, each contributing to a group mural. The therapist can suggest a theme, such as Scary

Monsters or What's Wrong with This Stupid School or What I Wish I Would Get for Christmas. Children then have the choice of participating in the group drawing or not, drawing something consistent with the theme or not, discussing the theme or not, all while the therapist engages each child in the interaction.

One interesting material to use for construction projects is food. Children can be nurtured with oral supplies and engaged in an interesting activity if they make their own peanut butter sandwiches or even bake their own cookies, where facilities permit. They can make faces on the sandwiches or squiggles on the cookies, lick jelly off their fingers or smear batter over their faces.

The physical activity of all these group games help children discharge energy and anxiety so that they can focus on the topics at hand and the other group members present in the room. It also means the group is fun! Children draw, cook, jump and dance, or move around the room playing roles while observing each other and acquiring the ability to interact more productively.


## CONCLUSION

This chapter has described the application of structured games to techniques of group therapy. Many of the therapeutic and expressive games used in individual treatment can be adapted for group work.

I believe that the structured play of board games, so necessary for individual therapy with latency-age children, is counterproductive to group treatment because each child's need to win and interest in cheating works against the other children's. If the board itself, and score-keeping and chip-collecting aspects can be left behind, activities that stimulate playful interaction can be used in the same way as all other play material. Like dramatic play and like the creative rule breaking of children at board games, expressive games can be seen as revealing information about the psychodynamics of group members.

Rules do exist because the children are in a group: they are asked to come in, sit down, do what others do, maintain appropriate boundaries, and interact with others. A group asks children to take turns and relate to others' turns, even if there is no board and no measured progress toward an end with winners and losers. Therefore, latency-age children's developmental needs for rules and structure are met within the group, and "cheating" can be seen in the way each group member accepts the group structure or rails against it. Refusing to sit on the chair or in the circle, wanting to take extra turns or "help" others with their turns, changing the subject away from the group discussion, and giggling and clowning at serious times are ways to "cheat" in group games. These methods of cheating can be understood the way creative board-game play can be understood in individual treatment, and the group can use symbolic material and expressive interaction as treatment.

# CHAPTER TEN

# Play Ball! . . . and Checkers, and Sorry, and Clue, and Monopoly, and . . .

Vinny sits on the couch, slumped down and staring at the floor. After a moment of strained silence, he says, "Wanna play a game?"

Tessa stands at length in front of the toy cupboard. She looks at all the toys, top to bottom. She touches some of them, then lets go. She remarks that she has toys like some of these, her school does, her friends do. Then she takes out Chutes and Ladders and starts the game.

Kenneth ignores the action figures and trucks and blocks he is said to play with at home. He climbs on a chair and reaches over his head for Sorry, dropping the other boxes in his attempt to get it down. He opens the box, sets up the board, then asks, "How do you play this game?"

Nadine plays out many dramatic scenes—with clay, animals, blocks, cars, dinosaurs, dishes and play food. One afternoon she puts the toys away, takes down Uno cards, and says, "My brother plays this game. Do you know how to play this game? Will you teach me how?"

Steve walks purposefully into the room, straight to the toy shelves. He reaches immediately for a board game—any board game, sets up the game without speaking, and begins to play. Once the play begins, he talks of his life at school and at home.

These children all show by the way they approach the playroom that they are ready, able, and needing to play board games. They clearly understand that there are other options—dramatic play or verbal interaction—and they may even use these options at other times or in other settings. Vinny and Steve try verbal therapy, but need board games to fill the time and ease their anxiety. Nadine plays dramatically and also wants to begin to learn board games, in the safe setting of therapy. Tessa and Kenneth look at the other toys but ignore them in their choice of board games exclusively.

Play with structured board games is developmentally appropriate for latency-age children but seldom discussed in the child therapy literature or seen as therapeutically useful. This book describes ways that structured board games can be seen to reveal children's psychodynamics, can be understood as projective material, and can be used therapeutically. If we watch carefully, we can find parallels between dramatic play and board-game play, in the way that both display the psychodynamics of the child who is playing, and we can use them in similar ways.

166

## CONCLUSION

Over the course of several years, latency-age children generally achieve a stage of development where they replace the dramatic, magical play of childhood with the structured, rule-oriented play of the middle years. In order to be successful therapists for children at this age, we must follow them in this development, rather than try to force them to continue with the more regressed play of childhood or to push them prematurely into the verbal world of adolescents and adults. We must learn to work with the material they give us, even when the material is expressed in the form of structured games.

I have tried to show here how the projective hypothesis of dramatic play and free association also applies to these structured games of latency. I have followed the treatment of two children whose therapy centered on structured games: aggressive Richard in Chapters 1 and 2, and compliant Adena in Chapter 7. If children are allowed to play creatively, bending and stretching and eliminating rules as they need to, their psychodynamics are revealed even in board games. If we watch for them, we can understand unconscious content, defensive needs, and interpersonal and transferential relationships in free play with structured games, just as well as with other symbolic material. We can then use that information in therapy with these children.

Our child patients of latency age have taken their turn, showing us that they prefer structured board games over dramatic play or talk; it is now our turn to learn how to play those games with them therapeutically.

167

# REFERENCES

Agre, L. G. (1997a). Bad dreams. In H. G. Kaduson & C. E. Schaefer (Eds.), *101 favorite play therapy techniques* (pp. 70–71). Northvale, NJ: Jason Aronson.

Agre, L. G. (1997b). Checkers: Rules or no rules. In H. G. Kaduson & C. E. Schaefer (Eds.), *101 favorite play therapy techniques* (pp. 137–138). Northvale, NJ: Jason Aronson.

Altman, N. (1997). The case of Ronald: Oedipal issues in the treatment of a seven-year-old boy. *Psychoanalytic Dialogues, 7,* 725–740.

Axline, V. (1969). *Play therapy.* New York: Ballantine.

Beiser, H. (1970). Children who cheat at games. *Journal of the American Academy of Child Psychiatry, 9,* 171–175.

Bellinson, J. (1991). Group psychotherapy with psychiatrically hospitalized children. In J. D. O'Brien, D. J. Pilowsky, & O. W. Lewis, *Psychotherapies with children and adolescents: Adapting the psychodynamic process* (pp. 313–335). Washington, DC: American Psychiatric Press.

Bellinson, J. (2000). Shut up and move: The uses of board games in child psychotherapy. *Journal of Infant, Child, and Adolescent Psychotherapy, 1*(2), 23–41.

Benedict, H. E. (1997). The feelings center. In H. G. Kaduson & C. E. Schaefer (Eds.), *101 favorite play therapy techniques* (pp. 383–387). Northvale, NJ: Jason Aronson.

Bixler, R. H. (1949). Limits are therapy. *Journal of Consulting Psychology, 13,* 1–11.

Blackwell, A. (1997). Create-a-puppet. In H. G. Kaduson & C. E. Schaefer (Eds.), *101 favorite play therapy techniques* (pp. 194–198). Northvale, NJ: Jason Aronson.

Boultinghouse, M. (1997). Puppetry. In H. G. Kaduson & C. E. Schaefer (Eds.), *101 favorite play therapy techniques* (pp. 204–208). Northvale, NJ: Jason Aronson.

Bromfield, R. (1997). *Playing for real: Exploring the world of child therapy and the inner worlds of children.* Northvale, NJ: Jason Aronson.

Brown, S. (1997). The photo album technique. In H. G. Kaduson & C. E. Schaefer (Eds.), *101 favorite play therapy techniques* (pp. 244–245). Northvale, NJ: Jason Aronson.

Cangelosi, D. (1997). Pounding away bad feelings. In H. G. Kaduson & C. E. Schaefer (Eds.), *101 favorite play therapy techniques* (pp. 142–144). Northvale, NJ: Jason Aronson.

Chethik, M. (1989). *Techniques of child therapy: Psychodynamic strategies.* New York: Guilford Press.

Cook, J. L. (1997a). The disposable camera technique. In H. G. Kaduson & C. E. Schaefer (Eds.), *101 favorite play therapy techniques* (pp. 388–390). Northvale, NJ: Jason Aronson.

Cook, J. L. (1997b). The dowel finger puppet technique. In H. G. Kaduson & C. E. Schaefer (Eds.), *101 favorite play therapy techniques* (pp. 191–193). Northvale, NJ: Jason Aronson.

Cook, J. L. (1997c). The time line tape technique. In H. G. Kaduson & C. E. Schaefer (Eds.), *101 favorite play therapy techniques* (pp. 372–374). Northvale, NJ: Jason Aronson.

Corder, B. F. (1986). Therapeutic games in group therapy with adolescents. In C. E. Schaefer & S. E. Reid (Eds.), *Game play:*

*Therapeutic uses of childhood games* (pp. 279–289). New York: John Wiley & Sons.

Coriat, I. H. (1941). The unconscious motives of interest in chess. *Psychoanalytic Review, 28,* 30–36.

Cunliffe, A. (1997). Therapeutic puppet group. In H. G. Kaduson & C. E. Schaefer (Eds.), *101 favorite play therapy techniques* (pp. 316–317). Northvale, NJ: Jason Aronson.

Davidson, P. (1997). The mad game. In H. G. Kaduson & C. E. Schaefer (Eds.), *101 favorite play therapy techniques* (pp. 191–193). Northvale, NJ: Jason Aronson.

Frederiksen, J. K. (1997). Storytelling with objects. In H. G. Kaduson & C. E. Schaefer (Eds.), *101 favorite play therapy techniques* (pp. 50–52). Northvale, NJ: Jason Aronson.

Freud, A. (1946). *The psychoanalytic treatment of children.* London: Imago.

Fried, S. (1992). Chess: A psychoanalytic tool in the treatment of children. *International Journal of Play Therapy, 1,* 43–51.

Gardner, J. E. (1993). Nintendo games. In C. E. Schaefer & D. M. Cangelosi (Eds.), *Play therapy techniques* (pp. 273–280). Northvale, NJ: Jason Aronson.

Gardner, R. A. (1971). *Therapeutic communication with children: The mutual storytelling technique.* New York: Jason Aronson.

Gardner, R. A. (1973). *The talking, feeling, doing game.* Cresskill, NJ: Creative Therapeutics. (8, 26, 27, 28, 30, 106, 109)

Gardner, R. A. (1975). *Psychotherapeutic approaches to the resistant child.* New York: Jason Aronson. (8, 21, 26, 30, 39, 106)

Gardner, R. A. (1983). The talking, feeling, and doing game. In C. E. Schaefer & K. J. O'Connor (Eds.), *Handbook of play therapy* (pp. 259–273). New York: John Wiley & Sons.

Gardner, R. A. (1993). Checkers. In C. E. Schaefer & D. M.

Cangelosi (Eds.), *Play therapy techniques* (pp. 247–262). Northvale, NJ: Jason Aronson.

Ginott, H. G. (1959). The theory and practice of "therapeutic intervention" in child treatment. *Journal of Consulting Psychology, 23,* 160–166.

Ginott, H. G. (1961). *Group psychotherapy with children.* New York: McGraw-Hill.

Ginott, H. G., & Lebo, D. (1962). Most and least used play therapy limits. *Journal of Genetic Psychology, 103,* 153–159.

Glatthorn, T. A. (1997). The anger shield. In H. G. Kaduson & C. E. Schaefer (Eds.), *101 favorite play therapy techniques* (pp. 272–275). Northvale, NJ: Jason Aronson.

Glenn, J. (Ed.). (1978). *Child analysis and therapy.* New York: Jason Aronson.

Harkin, M. J. (1997). Battaro and the puppet house. In H. G. Kaduson & C. E. Schaefer (Eds.), *101 favorite play therapy techniques* (pp. 185–190). Northvale, NJ: Jason Aronson.

Haworth, M. R. (Ed.). (1964). *Child psychotherapy.* New York: Basic Books.

Heidt, H. M. (1997). Using drawings of early recollections to facilitate life style analysis for children in play therapy. In H. G. Kaduson & C. E. Schaefer (Eds.), *101 favorite play therapy techniques* (pp. 327–332). Northvale, NJ: Jason Aronson.

Herman, J. L. (2000). Treating the cheater: An ego and self psychological approach to working through of the cheating syndrome in the treatment of latency children. *Journal of Infant, Child, and Adolescent Psychotherapy, 1*(2), 59–70.

Horn, T. (1997). Balloons of anger. In H. G. Kaduson & C. E. Schaefer (Eds.), *101 favorite play therapy techniques* (pp. 250–253). Northvale, NJ: Jason Aronson.

Jacobs, M. J. (1997). Mutual storytelling through puppet play in group play therapy. In H. G. Kaduson & C. E. Schaefer (Eds.), *101 favorite play therapy techniques* (pp. 320–324). Northvale, NJ: Jason Aronson.

Johnson, R. G. (1993). High-tech play therapy. In C. E. Schaefer & D. M. Cangelosi (Eds.), *Play therapy techniques* (pp. 281–286). Northvale, NJ: Jason Aronson.

Khan, M. R. (1983). From secretiveness to shared living. In *Hidden selves: Between theory and practice in psychoanalysis* (pp. 88–96). New York: International Universities Press.

Krimendahl, E. (2000). "Did you see that?": A relational perspective on children who cheat in analysis. *Journal of Infant, Child, and Adolescent Psychotherapy, 1*(2), 43–58.

Klein, M. (1932). *The psychoanalysis of children.* London: Hogarth Press.

Leonetti, J. (1997). Knocking down the walls of anger. In H. G. Kaduson & C. E. Schaefer (Eds.), *101 favorite play therapy techniques* (pp. 286–290). Northvale, NJ: Jason Aronson.

Levinson, B. M. (1976). Use of checkers in therapy. In C. E. Schaefer (Ed.), *The therapeutic use of child's play* (pp. 283–284). New York: Jason Aronson.

Loomis, E. A., Jr. (1964). The use of checkers in handling certain resistances in child therapy and child analysis. In M. R. Haworth (Ed.), *Child psychotherapy* (pp. 407–411). New York: Basic Books.

Matisse, C. (1997). On the one hand . . . and then on the other. In H. G. Kaduson & C. E. Schaefer (Eds.), *101 favorite play therapy techniques* (pp. 209–212). Northvale, NJ: Jason Aronson.

McDowell, B. (1997). The pick-up-sticks game. In H. G. Kaduson

& C. E. Schaefer (Eds.), *101 favorite play therapy techniques* (pp.145–149). Northvale, NJ: Jason Aronson.

Meagher, J. (1997). The angry feeling scale game. In H. G. Kaduson & C. E. Schaefer (Eds.), *101 favorite play therapy techniques* (pp. 281–282). Northvale, NJ: Jason Aronson.

Meeks, J. E. (1970). Children who cheat at games. *Journal of the American Academy of Child Psychiatry, 9,* 157–170.

Meeks, J. E. (1977). Structuring the early phase of group psychotherapy with adolescents. In J. F. McDermott & S. I. Harrison (Eds.), *Psychiatric treatment of the child* (pp. 487–503). New York: Jason Aronson.

Meeks, J. E. (2000). Reflections on children who cheat at games: A commentary. *Journal of Infant, Child, and Adolescent Psychotherapy, 1*(2), 71–75.

Moustakas, C. E. (1970). *Psychotherapy with children: The living relationship.* New York: Ballantine Books.

Narcavage, C. J. (1997). Using a puppet to create a symbolic client. In H. G. Kaduson & C. E. Schaefer (Eds.), *101 favorite play therapy techniques* (pp. 199–203). Northvale, NJ: Jason Aronson.

Oden, T. (1976). *The transactional analysis game.* New York: Harper & Row.

Peller, L. E. (1954). Libidinal phases, ego development, and play. *Psychoanalytic Study of the Child, 9,* 178–198.

Pitzen, K. (1997). My baby book. In H. G. Kaduson & C. E. Schaefer (Eds.), *101 favorite play therapy techniques* (pp. 343–346). Northvale, NJ: Jason Aronson.

Rachman, A. W. (1977). Encounter techniques in analytic group psychotherapy with adolescents. In J. F. McDermott & S. I.

Harrison, (Eds.), *Psychiatric treatment of the child* (pp. 471–478). New York: Jason Aronson.

Sands, R. M., & Golub, S. (1977). Breaking the bonds of tradition: A reassessment of group treatment of latency-age children. In J. F. McDermott & S. I. Harrison (Eds.), *Psychiatric treatment of the child* (pp. 479–486). New York: Jason Aronson.

Sarnoff, C. (1976). *Latency.* Northvale, NJ: Jason Aronson.

Saxe, S. (1997a). The angry tower. In H. G. Kaduson & C. E. Schaefer (Eds.), *101 favorite play therapy techniques* (pp. 246–249). Northvale, NJ: Jason Aronson.

Saxe, S. (1997b). Reworking. In H. G. Kaduson & C. E. Schaefer (Eds.), *101 favorite play therapy techniques* (pp. 97–99). Northvale, NJ: Jason Aronson.

Schaefer, C. E. (1997). The playing baby game. In H. G. Kaduson & C. E. Schaefer (Eds.), *101 favorite play therapy techniques* (pp. 3–5). Northvale, NJ: Jason Aronson.

Scheidlinger, S., & Rauch, E. (1972). Psychoanalytic group psychotherapy with children and adolescents. In B. B. Wolman (Ed.), *Handbook of child psychoanalysis* (pp. 364–398). New York: Van Nostrand Reinhold.

Schmidt, M. M. (1997). The twelve-to-one technique. In H. G. Kaduson & C. E. Schaefer (Eds.), *101 favorite play therapy techniques* (pp. 362–365). Northvale, NJ: Jason Aronson.

Shaw, L. N. (1998). A boy in analysis. *Journal of Clinical Psychoanalysis, 7,* 445–471.

Short, A. H. (1997). Inner-reference. In H. G. Kaduson & C. E. Schaefer (Eds.), *101 favorite play therapy techniques* (pp. 93–96). Northvale, NJ: Jason Aronson.

Short, G. F. (1997a). Art or verbal metaphors for children experiencing loss. In H. G. Kaduson & C. E. Schaefer (Eds.), *101 favorite play therapy techniques* (pp. 40–43). Northvale, NJ: Jason Aronson.

Short, G. F. (1997b). Group puppet show. In H. G. Kaduson & C. E. Schaefer (Eds.), *101 favorite play therapy techniques* (pp. 318–319). Northvale, NJ: Jason Aronson.

Short, G. F. (1997c). Life maps. In H. G. Kaduson & C. E. Schaefer (Eds.), *101 favorite play therapy techniques* (pp. 77–79). Northvale, NJ: Jason Aronson.

Siepker, B. B., & Kandaras, C. S. (Eds.). (1985). *Group therapy with children and adolescents: A treatment manual.* New York: Human Sciences Press.

Slade, A., & Wolf, D. P. (Eds.). (1994). *Children at play: Clinical and developmental approaches to meaning and representation.* New York: Oxford University Press.

Slavson, S. R. (1943). *An introduction to group therapy.* New York: International Universities Press.

Slavson, S. R. (1955). Criteria for selection and rejection of patients for various types of group psychotherapy. *International Journal of Group Psychotherapy, 5,* 3–30.

Slavson S. R., & Schiffer, M. (1975). *Group psychotherapies for children.* New York: International Universities Press.

Smith, W. H. (1993). Chess. In C. E. Schaefer & D. M. Cangelosi (Eds.), *Play therapy techniques* (pp. 263–270). Northvale, NJ: Jason Aronson.

Solnit, A. J., & Neubauer, P.B. (Eds.). (1987). *Psychoanalytic Study of the Child, 42,* 3–219.

Spiegel, S. (1996). *An interpersonal approach to child and adolescent psychotherapy.* Northvale, NJ: Jason Aronson.

Sugar, M. (1974). Interpretive group psychotherapy with latency children. *Journal of the American Academy of Child Psychiatry, 13,* 648–666.

Tierney, C. G. (1997). Jenga and a camera. In H. G. Kaduson & C. E. Schaefer (Eds.), *101 favorite play therapy techniques* (pp. 268–271). Northvale, NJ: Jason Aronson.

Van Scoy, H. (1971). An activity group approach to severely disturbed latency boys. *Child Welfare, 50,* 413–419.

Van Scoy, H. (1977). Activity group therapy: A bridge between play and work. In J. F. McDermott & S. I. Harrison (Eds.), *Psychiatric treatment of the child* (pp. 461–469). New York: Jason Aronson.

Winnicott, D. W. (1977). *The piggle: An account of the psychoanalytic treatment of a little girl.* New York: International Universities Press.

Wunderlich, C. (1997). Stomping feet and bubble popping. In H. G. Kaduson & C. E. Schaefer (Eds.), *101 favorite play therapy techniques* (pp. 283–285). Northvale, NJ: Jason Aronson.

Zalick, R. (1975). *The ungame.* Anaheim, CA: Ungame.

Zelnick, L. (1999). Contribution to P. Carnochan (Ed.), A forum on child analysis and play therapy. *Psychologist/Psychoanalyst, 19*(1), 22–25.

Board games *(continued)*
  and use in psychiatric
    hospitals, 147
  as used by boys, 115–116
  as used by girls, 115–116
Boggle, 18
Box of Words game, 155

Candyland, 67, 93–96, 105,
    107, 138
Cards, 18
Charades in group therapy,
    158–161
Cheating, 7, 12, 25–27 *See Also*
    Board games, cheating at
  as creative play, 63, 71–72,
    74–75, 83, 112–114,
    129–130, 135
  disallowed by therapist, 71
  discussing with child, 27–30,
    84
  getting away with, 68
  interpretation of, 67–68, 73,
    83–84
  and lack of need to, 69–71
  permitted by therapist, 94–
    95, 129
  productive use of in therapy,
    60
  styles of, 64–68

length of time engaging in,
    66–67, 69–70
  within the rules, 117–118
Checkers, 5, 75, 90–91, 134,
    137
Chess, 6–11, 18, 21, 26, 28–
    31, 138
Child therapy
  literature on play in, 3–5
Chutes and Ladders, 59, 64,
    82–83, 105, 110, 114,
    138, 165
Clue, 4, 17–19, 75
Confrontation of issues, 52
Connect Four, 95

Dramatic play
  control of in therapy, 61–62
  developmental movement
    away from, 4–5, 12–
    13, 19
  examples of, 8, 11, 17
  information gleaned from, 8
  interpretation of, 2
  literature regarding, 3
  themes emergent in struc-
    tured, 2, 13

Fair play, 12, 25–26, 31, 60–
    61, 78, 127

children who practice, 69–
    71, 72–73
Feelings
    dealing with in group therapy,
        153–157
Finger paint, 21

Games
    board, 2–3
    child's choice of, 19–22,
        96–97
    child-provided, 22–25
    electronic, 22–25
    focused play of, 82–84
    of luck, 137–138
    of skill, 137–138
    structured, 2–3
Gardner, Richard, 6, 8, 34,
    37–38, 152, 155
Go, 18
Go Fish, 92–93
Group therapy
    activities for, 161–162
    anger dealt with in, 156–157
    examples of non-board games
        for use in, 150–161
    feelings dealt with in,
        153–157
    goal of leader in, 161
    and non-winner games, 147,
        149

role-playing in, 158–161
rules applicable to, 163
and severely disturbed
    children, 148
use of Bag of Things game
    in, 152–155
use of board games in, 145–
    148, 162–163
use of Box of Words game
    in, 155
use of Charades in, 158–161
use of non-board games in,
    149–150
use of Pitcher of Feelings
    game in, 155–157
use of Talking, Feeling,
    Doing game in,
    149–152

Headache, 61

Interactional Analysis Game,
    7–8, 34

Khan, Masud, 7

Latency-age children
    play of, 4–5
    and talk therapy, 33, 55
    tasks of, 4, 12–13, 25–26

## About the Author

Jill Bellinson, Ph.D. is a faculty member and supervisor at the William Alanson White Institute, the Metropolitan Institute for Training in Psychoanalytic Psychotherapy, and the National Institute for the Psychotherapies. She has played board games with children in therapy for more than 20 years, most recently in private practice in New York City.